Ultimate Beginner Tech Start

Live Sound Basics

MW00666912

By Tony Marvuglio

Alfred
Alfred Music Publishing Co., Inc.
P.O. Box 10003
Van Nuys, CA 91410-0003
alfred.com

ISBN-10: 0-7692-9055-8
ISBN-13: 978-0-7692-9055-3

Dedication & Thanks

This book is dedicated to my wife Debbie and my sons Shane and Anthony.
Their constant love, support, and confidence continually help
me attain new levels personally and professionally.
Special thanks to Debbie Cavalier, David Mash,
Barry Doubleday, and Bruce Bennett for their
support and guidance in this project.

Contents

Introduction

Do you know that P.A. stands for Public Address system? Do you know what a mixer is used for? Are you wondering if you should buy an integrated or a component system for your band? Are you confused by the different types of microphones? Do you think a polar pattern is a weather graph of the North and South Poles? If any of these questions have entered your mind, this guide is designed to help you.

New technologies continue to make improvements in the equipment used in P.A. systems, but the basics remain the same: you need to mix together microphone (informally called "mike" and abbreviated as "mic" on most equipment) and instrument signals, amplify them, and deliver the sound to your audience through a set of loudspeakers.

Some considerations when buying or renting a sound system are:

1. How many instruments and microphones will be plugged into the P.A.?
   This will determine the type and size of mixer.
2. In what size rooms will your band normally play?
   This will determine speaker size, amplifier (amp) power, and possibly some signal processing.
3. How loudly do you need to play?
   Will you be plugging low-frequency instruments like bass guitar and synthesizers into your P.A.? Amp power and speaker size come into play here. And remember, unless you're lucky enough to have roadies, you will be the one lifting and transporting the gear.

Throughout this guide, two terms will be used quite often: *signal* and *sound*. It is important to understand the differences between them as applied to sound reinforcement. Even though you can hear a vocalist sing through a microphone, the mixer receives the mike's electronic output voltage (the signal), not the sound. A small voltage is produced by the output of the mike when sound causes its diaphragm to move a coil within a magnetic field. (This is called transduction.) This signal passes from the mike's output into the mixer's input and is processed by the different mixer sections. This signal then passes from the mixer to the amplifier. The amplified signal is what moves the cones in the speakers and reproduces the original sound from the microphone at a louder level. Of course, this is an overly simplified explanation of what happens, but if you understand how the sound becomes an electronic signal and then converts back to sound, you are well on your way to effectively setting up and operating a sound system or P.A. Understanding signal flow is the single most important thing for using and troubleshooting today's modern P.A.s. Ultimately, by reading this book, you will be able to make sense of the different types of equipment specifications used in a sound system, make good judgments when selecting your gear, and connect and use it all effectively.

Chapter One

What Is Sound Reinforcement?

The basic premise of sound reinforcement is to bring the band's sound level up above the ambient room sound so it can be heard. Ambient room sound is the noise caused by things like conversations, cash registers, and air conditioners. Sound reinforcement is achieved through the use of microphones, mixers, signal processing, power amps, and speakers. I will take you through the different pieces that make up a modern P.A. system and give you some practical applications for operating a sound system in a live performance situation.

System Types

There are two types of sound systems: integrated and component. Both have advantages and disadvantages, but choosing the right type for your needs is essential. If you play small clubs with a trio, you will probably need an integrated system. On the other hand, if you play in a number of different room sizes with medium to large groups, you'll need to invest in a component system. You may even need to buy a couple of different speaker size combinations to accommodate the various places you play. I remember bringing a P.A. to a gig only to find out there wasn't enough room on the stage, floor, or any place else for the large speakers. One more thing—don't expect a club owner to give up customer seating so you can put your speakers on the tables.

The Integrated System

An integrated or self-contained system is one in which the mixer and amplifier are boxed as a single unit and often includes a set of speakers. This type of system is compact and requires little set-up.

An integrated system, shown in Figure 1 on the next page, is usually a box with mike and line inputs as well as basic controls such as a mike or line input, volume control, monitor/auxiliary send, and high and low equalization (known as EQ) on each channel. (EQ is a sophisticated type of tone control.) Sometimes a graphic equalizer is included in the main output section to allow for the overall tonal balance of the speaker's sound. The amplifier is built into the unit, so no additional connections are necessary from the mixer. You just need to plug in your mikes and instruments, set the levels, add some EQ (if necessary), connect the speakers, and you're ready to go. The main limitation of the integrated system is that it usually has only six or eight inputs, but for small groups, solo performers, and duos that shouldn't be a problem. The advantage of the integrated sound system is its small size. If the room is small enough and you're not using stage monitors, the main unit and two speakers are all you'll need to bring to your gig.

Another version of the integrated system, as seen in Figure 1, offers a full feature mixer with an integrated power amp. This is basically the same as the component system since the mixer will offer a greater amount of signal routing and flexibility. The only difference is that a separate power amp is not necessary.

Peavey X600E Integrated Amp

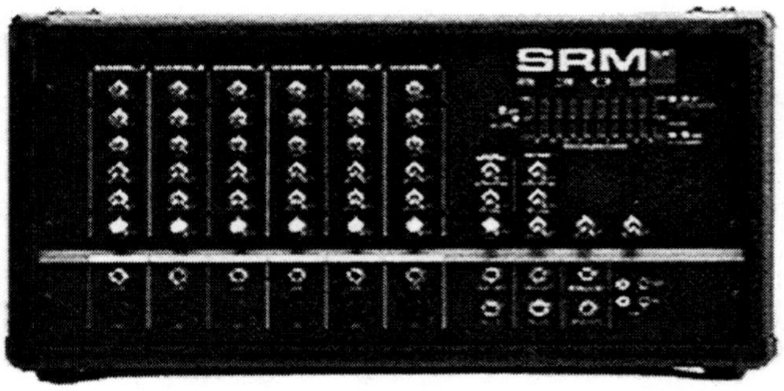

Fender SRM Integrated Mixer/Amp

Figure 1: Integrated Amp (top) and Mixer/Amp (bottom)

The Component System

The component system is made by combining individual units: mixer, power amp(s), signal processors, and speakers. It offers the greatest amount of flexibility, and it is also the most complicated to set up and operate. Each item in the system must be compatible and connected in a specific and exact order. A big advantage of this system is that it can be upgraded easily; any component can be added or replaced at any time.

Chapter Two

Mixers

The mixer is sometimes referred to by other names: console, board, or desk. The mixer is the component that has microphone and line inputs (where you plug in the mike or instrument cables). It is capable of adjusting the signal's volume, tonal characteristics (EQ), pan (position in the stereo field from left to right), and routing. Routing is when you send the signal to a specific output such as the main, stage monitor, and aux (auxiliary) outs. Using a mixer can be intimidating sometimes because of the amount of knobs and sliders on it. However, if we break down each area of the mixer into sections according to their functions, operating it becomes manageable.

There are many features and options available on today's modern mixers. Careful consideration of your needs in advance will save you time and money. Nothing is more frustrating than trying to make a mixer do something it was not designed for. For example, if you are planning to record your band live from the P.A., make sure your mixer has tape outputs.

Mixers are referred to by the number of inputs, submaster outputs, and stereo or mono outputs. For instance, a 12 x 4 x 2 mixer would have 12 inputs, 4 submaster outputs, and 2 outputs (a stereo pair). Before making any purchases, determine the minimum number of inputs you need: Will you need to send submixes to monitors or tape decks? Will the final mix to the house main speaker system be in stereo or mono?

Another pre-purchase consideration is the number of auxiliary (aux) sends available. Aux sends can be either pre- or post-EQ. This is important if you want to use one of these sends for your stage monitor amps and speakers.

Sometimes the number of inputs available can be confusing. A mixer may be a 12-input mixer but may not have 12 discreet inputs. This may or may not be a big issue, but it is certainly one to consider. Many mixers have a combination of mono and stereo inputs; with this configuration you will not be able to plug in 12 separate instruments or mikes. The reason is that the stereo inputs are controlled by a single input channel. You certainly can plug a single mike or instrument into these channels, but it limits your total amount of mono inputs to 8 instead of 12. These inputs are normally used for plugging in the stereo outputs of a submixer, a keyboard, or other stereo instrument.

There are mixers, like the one in Figure 2, that are designed specifically for live sound reinforcement, but most multipurpose mixers will do the job well. In considering what mixer to buy, you'll have to ask yourself what the mixer will need to do. If you will be doing multitrack recording, you probably will be better off with a mixer designed for that purpose since it will be easier to adapt it to live use. Since mixers designed for recording normally have a number of different ways to route the signals, you'll have the flexibility you'll need to send signals to monitor mixes and auxiliary outputs for signal processing. A live console, on the other hand, may not have all of the signal routing necessary to send to individual tracks of a recorder.

Figure 2: Mackie SR24 Sound Reinforcement Mixer

Inputs

Now it's time to get into a little wirehead talk. Have you ever read the specifications in the back of the mixer's manual? If not, the input part reads something like this: Maximum levels mic in: +14 dB; Impedance mic in: 1.3 kilohms. Let's break this down into understandable terms. The first part, *maximum level mic in*, is concerned with the amount of signal applied to the input. Compare this to a rush of water flowing down a river; as long as the water stays within the river's banks, the countryside is safe. The maximum signal level coming into the mixer's input (the river) can't exceed a certain level (the river's banks) or it will distort and cause horrible sounds to come from your speaker system (the river overflowing its banks). Mike inputs and associated pre-amps are capable of handling very low voltage levels from a microphone and boosting them to a usable level. If you use too much boost or have a hot signal come in to this input, you won't like what you hear. When setting levels for microphones, make sure that the volume is all the way down. Then have the vocalist sing into the mike or have the instrumentalist play something. During this process, slowly bring up the volume until the sound is as loud as possible without distorting.

The second part, *impedance mic in*, refers to the resistance of the electrical circuit. Think of impedance as a dam holding back the river. As long as the dam (the impedance) is strong enough to hold back the river (the microphone), they are evenly matched. The rule here is that the mixer's input impedance should be higher than the impedance rating of the microphone. In modern mixers, this is usually not a problem since the input impedance is high enough to accept anything from microphones to electronic keyboards. Follow this simple rule and all will be cool.

And, finally, for those of you who want to have the technical information, here's the scoop: dB stands for *decibel*, which is the unit of measurement of an audio signal level in an electrical circuit, referenced to 0.775 VRMS (volt root means square) into any impedance. This is normally used to describe signal levels in most audio systems.

A kilohm is 1,000 ohms, which is a unit of measurement of electrical resistance to current flow.

Since this guide is really meant to get you using the equipment, I'll bring up this sort of technical information only when it is absolutely necessary.

Balanced Versus Unbalanced lines

So, what does all of this mean and how important is it? Well, if you are running long cables (over 25 feet) to your mixer, it's very important. Although I could give a long explanation of the characteristics of these types of lines, it is sufficient to say that, overall, balanced lines offer better noise rejection. What kinds of noises induce a hum in a P.A. system that is unbearable to both the musicians and the audience? The most common are ground loops, electromagnetic interference (EMI), and radio frequency interference (RFI). Higher noise rejection is due to the way balanced lines handle the signal. A sound passing across the mike's diaphragm creates an analogous (same as the original sound) signal at the mike output that has both a positive and negative polarity. Look at Figure 3 to see how the sine wave form moves from zero voltage up to a maximum point, goes back to zero, and then progresses to a point that is the negative equivalent of the original positive pass.

The height or intensity of the wave from zero to the maximum point is amplitude. In a balanced line, two separate cables are used to carry each of these signals (one positive [+] and one negative [-]). This creates a strong, clean signal, and cable lengths can be much longer. The ground is the third cable in the balanced line. It is the point of zero voltage in a circuit and is the point by which other voltages are measured. This cable also provides a path that connects to a safety ground on the chassis of the mixer. An electrical device that has a safety ground circuit has a three-prong connector with two flat blades and a rounded plug that fits into the wall. Don't ever break off the rounded ground plug from your power cable or defeat its purpose by using an adapter. It is called a SAFETY GROUND for a reason. The reason is that the rounded plug provides a path of lower resistance than you or the musicians to ground. If you remove this plug, you may become the path of least resistance, and the electrical system will pass through you as a ground. Yikes!

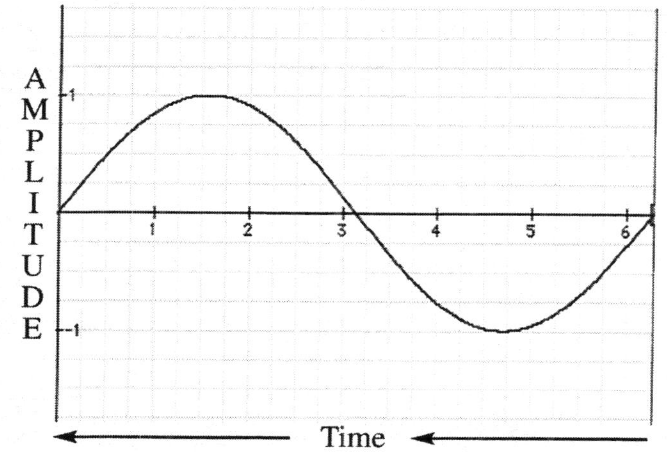

One full cycle from zerp, through positive amplitude,
back to zero, through negative amplitude, and back to zero

Figure 3: Sine Wave

Mic/XLR

The XLR or Cannon connector is the most common low-impedance microphone cable connector used today. It is a three-pin connector that carries positive and negative audio signals and a ground or cable shield. The balanced configuration connects the ground or cable shield to Pin 1, the positive audio cable to Pin 2, and the negative audio cable to Pin 3. The unbalanced configuration connects the negative and ground or cable shields together, then solders to Pins 1 and 3, and connects the positive audio signal to Pin 2. The XLR connector also has a locking pin that secures it to the mike and mixer. Some individuals remove the locking pin from the mixer to allow for easy and quick disconnections. The rule of thumb for XLR connectors is that female connectors are inputs and male connectors are outputs.

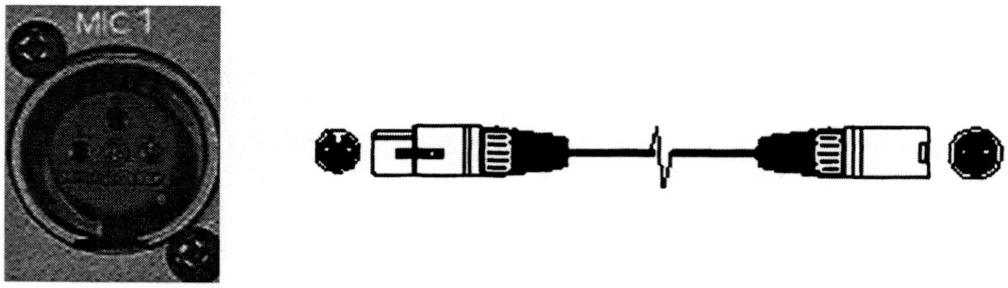

Figure 4: XLR Microphone input connector (Mackie) and XLR cable (SoundCraft Illustration)

Line / 1/4"

This input usually has a 1/4" female phone jack connector that accepts a male 1/4" phone plug (typical on most electronic instruments). Most of us know this as a guitar cable. In its unbalanced configuration, it uses a tip/sleeve connection, which is the phone plug that has two parts separated by a plastic ring. The tip, which carries the positive (+) signal, has an indentation to lock into the female connector. The sleeve is the longer barrel portion of the connector and is connected to the ground or shield of the cable.

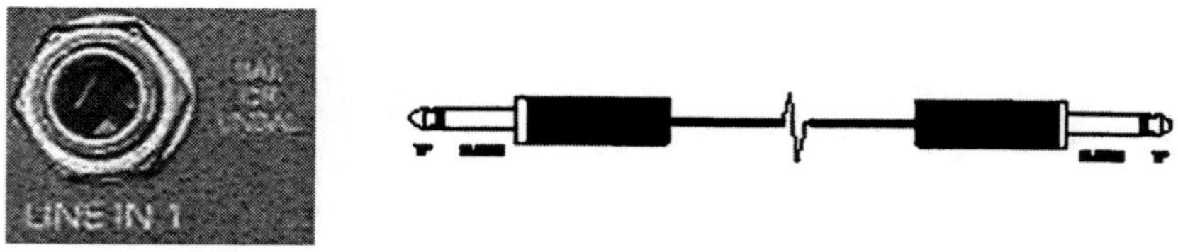

Figure 5: 1/4" Line input jack and 1/4" TS unbalanced phone plug

In its balanced configuration, this plug uses a tip/ring/sleeve connection and each part is separated by a plastic ring. There are three wires in the cable instead of two. The tip is connected to the positive (+) signal, the ring to the negative (-), and the sleeve to the shield or ground. This is typically used by electronic instruments such a synthesizers or electric pianos. However, you must check the owner's manuals on these instruments to see if they support balanced lines. The female connection has three parts that connect to the appropriate section of the phone plug.

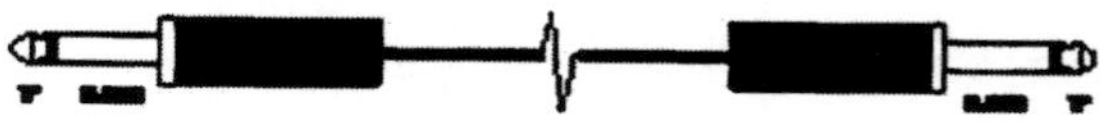

Figure 6: TRS balanced 1/4" phone plug

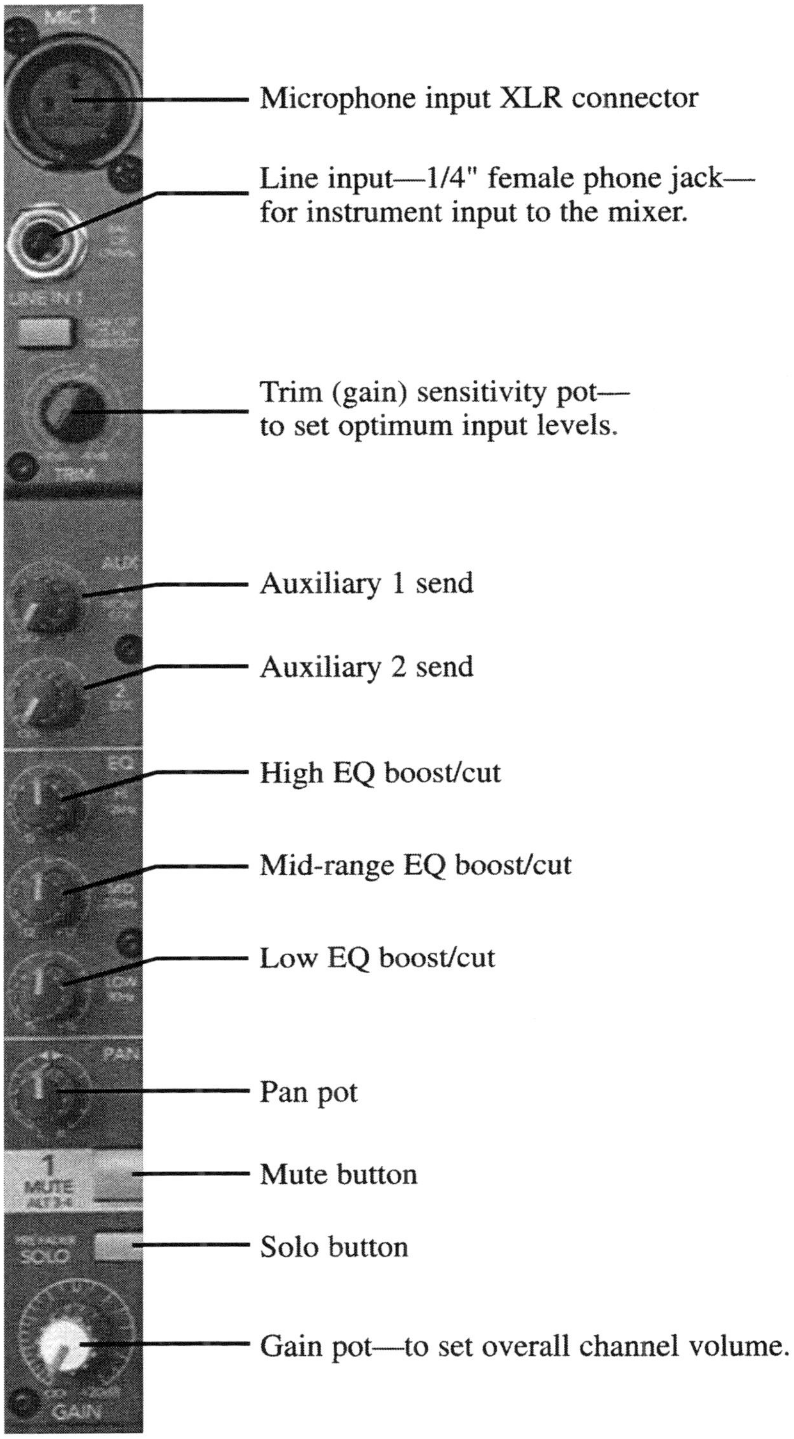

Figure 7: Input channel module Mackie 1202-VLZ mixer

Trim/Gain/Sensitivity

These three terms are sometimes used interchangeably, but I'll use *sensitivity* here to avoid confusion with the channel volume fader or the gain potentiometer (called a *pot* for short) discussed later. Sensitivity has to do with how input deals with incoming signals. This rotary control lets you set the optimal level for the mike inputs. Mixers vary in their settings for this control. Some have an overload LED (light emitting diode) on the channel. To set sensitivity on them, apply a signal to the input and increase the gain until the overload LED flashes. Then back off the sensitivity control lightly, and optimum levels are set. Another mixer manufacturer uses the solo button on the channel to assist in setting sensitivity. In this case, set your levels by first inserting a mike or instrument into the input channel, and then engage the solo button. Turn the sensitivity control until the meters read 0 VU while you apply a signal. For example, sing into the mike or play something on your instrument. It is important to set this control to optimize the signal-to-noise ratio of the mixer. All mixers have inherent noise based on the fact that electricity generates heat as it passes through components. By optimizing the signal coming into the mixer (setting it at its maximum level), the noise generated by the mixer is "masked" or covered up and no longer factors in the sound sent to the P.A. amps.

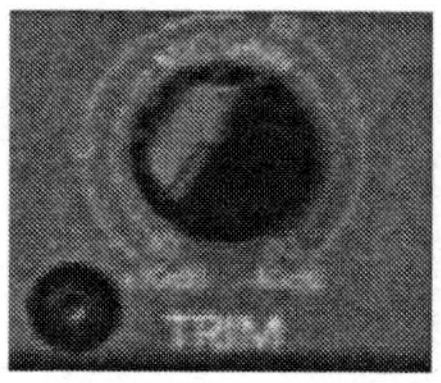

Figure 8: Mackie (Sensitivity) Trim Pot

EQ (Equalizer)

What exactly does an equalizer do? It allows control over the tonal characteristics of a signal. Hertz is a unit of measurement for audio frequencies and is abbreviated Hz. One hertz is a signal or sound oscillating at one cycle per second. Human hearing can perceive frequencies from 20 Hz to 20,000 Hz, approximately ten musical octaves. Let's put this in musical terms. If you pick the fifth string of a guitar, that note, the low A, should be tuned to 220 Hz. That means the string and subsequent sound are oscillating 220 times per second. This is well within the audible range of human hearing. Cut that sound in half and you get the third string of a bass guitar, the low A; it now vibrates at 110 cycles per second, still well in the range of our hearing. Cut that in half and now you hear and feel 55 cycles per second, which is the low A produced by the pedals of a pipe organ. As we get older, most of us lose our high-frequency hearing in the top range where sound oscillates at 20,000 times per second. If you are exposed to very loud sounds on a regular basis, the high-frequency range in your hearing will normally be the first you lose.

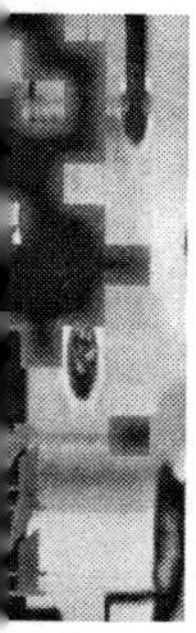

Another characteristic of human hearing is that we don't hear all frequencies equally at the same volume. Our hearing is most acute in the mid-range frequencies. A typical application is the telephone. At low volumes, our hearing is less sensitive to the low and high frequencies. Since our voices are primarily in the mid-ranges, we don't need to have a full range of frequencies on the phone. As the volume increases, we have a tendency to hear all of the frequencies more equally. This is why the sound of a band can lose its punch when a club owner tells it to turn down the volume. We'll discuss setting levels to overcome this obstacle in the Practical Applications section.

Now back to the equalizer. As I said earlier, this control changes the low, mid-range, and high-frequency characteristics of a signal. This pot normally has a center indent (usually at 12 o'clock), which means no EQ is being applied. As the pot is rotated clockwise, that frequency range is increased or boosted. If the pot is rotated counterclockwise, that range is decreased or cut. Some modern mixers feature sweepable low- and high-frequency pots and a selectable mid-range set of pots. One mid-range pot is for the frequency and the other is for boost or cut.

Figure 9 shows a set of sweepable EQ pots. The frequencies are fixed (preset at the factory during manufacture) so you cannot cut or boost specific frequencies.

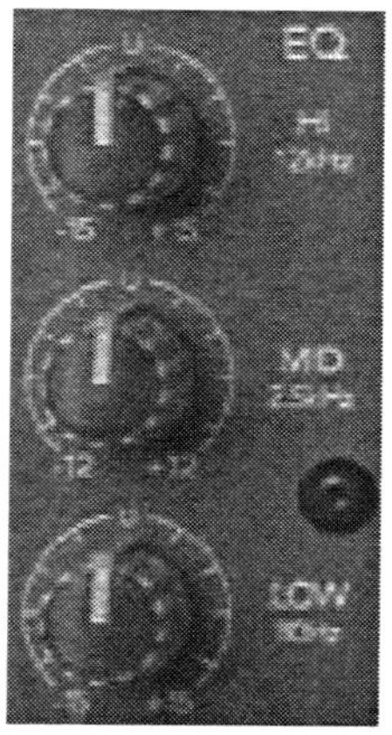

Figure 9: Mackie 1202 VLZ Sweepable EQ

Figure 10 shows an EQ system with sweepable high and low EQ pots and a selectable mid-range set of pots. This offers greater flexibility in controlling the mid-range equalization of a signal.

Usually, if you are equalizing signals to sound good in the main speakers, you will create feedback in the stage monitors. Feedback is a rumble, low howl, or high-pitched squeal that is caused when the output of a speaker is picked up by a microphone, fed back through the system, amplified, and re-sent to the speaker system. This cycle continues until it produces the unwanted sound in the system. If you set the EQ to sound good in the stage monitors, the main speaker systems may sound too muddy. By defeating the EQ to the monitors, you can get a good sound in the main speakers and use an outboard graphic or parametric EQ to adjust the sound in the monitors. Additionally, if you want to use aux sends for reverbs and other signal processing, you may need more than two available aux sends on the mixer.

Figure 10: Illustration of Mackie Selectable Mid-Range EQ

Aux (Auxiliary) Sends

These pots (Figure 11) are linked to a coinciding output for sending the signal to monitor amps or signal processing equipment independent of the main mixer outs. Remember that we're processing the signal here, not the sound. This section of a mixer can be used to send a signal to an amp to power the stage monitors so you can hear the band mix. It also provides a way to send signals independently to reverbs, delays, or other outboard signal processing equipment if a special effect is required for that instrument or mike.

These sends are either pre- or post-fader or pre- or post-EQ. If the send is pre-fader, the overall level can be set independently of the fader position. This is useful if you want to send a drum machine count-off to your monitors but not to the main mix. In this case, the rim shot from the drum machine is fed into an input, but the fader is set so no level is sent to the main speaker system. The aux send feeding the monitor amp is then brought up to a level so you can hear the count-off on stage but not over the main speaker system. If the aux send is post-fader, then the fader controlling the channel level will also affect the signal sent to the monitor amp. This also holds true for pre- and post-EQ. If the send is pre-EQ, then the equalization set in the channel is not sent to the monitor amp. Pre-fader and pre-EQ are the most useful settings for driving stage monitors. By using aux sends in this way, you can create a mix in the monitors that is independent of what is sent to the main power amp and speaker system.

Post-fader and post-EQ are usually used when driving external signal processing such as reverb. The reason for this is that the signal is routed from the aux send to the reverb and the processed (wet) sound is returned to the mixer and combined with the original (dry) signal. This allows you to mix dry and wet signals proportionately so that they sound pleasing and realistic. If you use pre-fader aux sends and need to fade out the original signal in that channel, the reverb (wet) sound is still in the main speakers with no original (dry) signal. Although this has been used as a special effect in some circumstances, it is rarely used as the main sound setting in a P.A. system.

Figure 11: Mackie Aux Sends

Pan (Stereo) Pot

A panoramic potentiometer (Figure 12) allows you to move a monophonic signal through a continuous range (left, right, and center) in the stereo field. To place an instrument hard left of center, for example, turn this knob fully counterclockwise. You can place any instrument variably through 180° in the stereo spectrum with this control.

On mixers with stereo input channels, this pot is normally set in the center position. This allows the stereo signal fed at the input to be panned externally by the device.

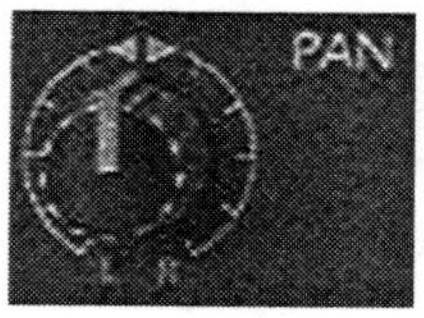

Figure 12: Mackie Pan Pot

Mute Button

When the mute button is depressed, the signal coming into the input of the channel cannot pass through to the various outputs of the mixer. It is like disconnecting the cable from the input or turning down the fader and all of the pre- and post-fader sends. This is handy to remove signals from the mix during performance and sound checks.

Solo Button

The solo button is used to monitor a single channel. When this button is depressed, all the other incoming signals are muted and only the channel(s) that are soloed are sent to the solo monitor of the mixer. This is very handy for listening to selected input channels.

In addition, on some mixers (Mackies in particular) the solo button is used in conjunction with the sensitivity pot to set a channel's optimum operating level. To set levels on a Mackie mixer, you connect a mike to the channel input and depress the solo button. While singing into the mike, increase the sensitivity pot until the level LED meters read approximately 0 VU. Once you do this, disengage the solo button, and the proper input level is set.

Fader or Volume

This is the audio level control for the channel, and depending on its type, it will be a fader or pot. A fader is a slider control (it slides up and down) that provides the boost or cut of a channel's audio signal. *Fade-out* results from gradually sliding this control down until the audio signal is not heard anymore.

If this control is a pot, it is a rotary knob that allows for continuous cut or boost from left to right. Turning this knob clockwise will result in a higher audio signal (louder sound). Turning it counter-clockwise will make the audio signal lower (softer or no sound).

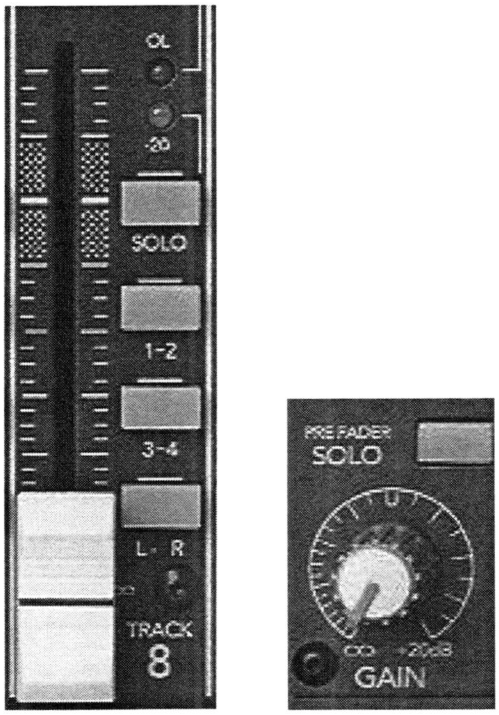

Figure 13: Mackie Volume Fader and Potentiometer (Pot)

Outputs

Mixer outputs are used to get the signal to a useful point. Possible destinations are power amps, signal processors, stage monitor power amps, or tape decks. No, I'm not going to give you the whole output wirehead story like I did with inputs. However, as with inputs, you have to match outputs to the corresponding destination's inputs (usually a power amp). This is referenced by +4 dB or -10 dB. Using the water analogy again, think of the +4 version as a big water pipe with a lot of water coming down it. If the input pipe is also a +4 dB, it can handle all the water, and the flow is smooth without backups or overload. So, if you connect a +4 dB output to a +4 dB input, your sound will be nice and smooth. But if you connect a +4 dB output to a -10 dB input, you will overload the pipe. The amp's input will overload and the sound will be distorted. If you match a -10 dB output to a +4 dB input, the signal will be too low. M atch up the pipes for best performance. Your owner's manual will give you the specs.

Main Outs (Main Mix)

These sets of jacks send the signal from the mixer to the main amplifier. There are two types of jacks typically used for the main outs: XLR and 1/4" phone jacks. As with the inputs, the XLR jacks usually carry a +4 dB signal and the 1/4" phone jacks carry a -10 dB. Notice I said *usually*. You should check the unit's specifications to find out to what level a particular set of output jacks send. It is important to match the output of the mixer with the input of the amplifier to achieve the best signal-to-noise ratio or to eliminate unwanted distortion.

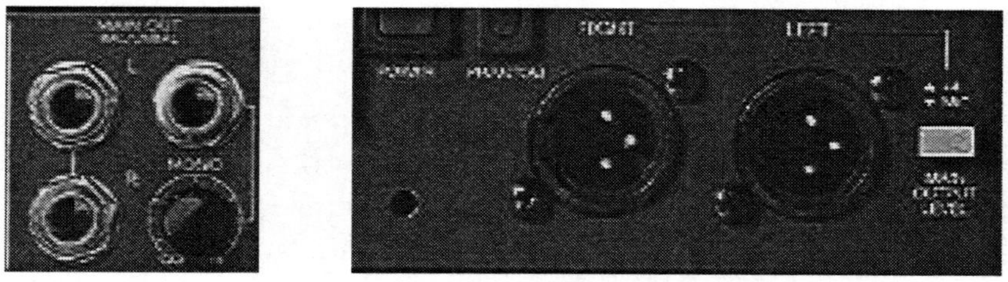

Figure 14: Main Output Jacks on a Mackie 1604 and a 1202-VLZ Mixer

Auxiliary (Aux) Outs

This output is used in conjunction with the aux send pot in the channel input section of the mixer. The aux outs are used to send signals out of the mixer to a number of different destinations. One of these sends can be used to send signals to the stage monitor amp. Another can be used to route signals to outboard equipment like digital delays, reverbs, and other signal processors. The amount of external routing on a mixer is associated directly with the number of aux send outputs available.

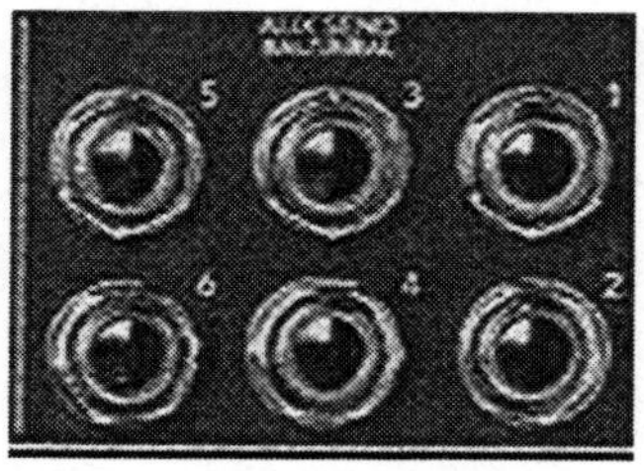

Figure 15: Aux Send Jacks on a Mackie 1604 Mixer

Sub-Outputs

This group of controls is not available on every mixer, but many multipurpose mixers that are used for recording and sound reinforcement have them. The sub-outs are a group of faders and associated output jacks. They allow the user to assign a number of input channels to a sub-group and then use the master subfaders to control the overall volume of the group. A typical use is to control the volume of a drum set. For instance, the drums' mikes are using channels 6 through 12. Channel 6 is the kick drum, channel 7 is the snare drum, channel 8 is the hi-hat, channels 9 and 10 are toms, and channels 11 and 12 are the overheads for cymbals. Once the levels are set for each channel, they are not assigned to the left and right mains but to the sub-out 1. Then the sub-out 1 master fader is assigned to the left and right main outs. In this way, the single sub-out 1 fader can control the balanced volumes of the entire drum set with one fader. This can be done with other groups like vocals or keyboards by following the same procedure and assigning them to a different sub-out fader.

Monitor Section

Before I explain the monitor section, here's a quick word about buses. A bus is an electrical circuit that combines many signals and routes them to a specific destination. The main mix bus contains all of the channel input signals that are assigned to the main mix outs. Likewise, the Aux 1 send bus contains the combined signals of all the input channels that use the Aux 1 send pot and appear at the Aux 1 outs.

The monitor section of the mixer is comprised of selector switches and a volume control or fader. By selecting a specific section, the engineer can monitor the different output buses of the mixer through headphones or external speakers. For instance, if the main mix is selected, the signal as it appears at the input of the amplifier is sent to the headphones. Likewise, the engineer can monitor any signal coming from the mixer to check for distortion and overall balance. A small set of powered speakers can be connected to the monitor outputs of the mixer. The engineer can use these small speakers for listening during set-up instead of headphones. It is very common to listen to the aux bus that feeds external signal processing equipment. By monitoring the different output buses, the engineer can make sure that a clean signal is feeding the inputs of the various devices.

Somewhere on the console is a set of meters. LED (see Figure 16) meters are the most common meters on current models. However, the older style VU (volume unit) meters do show up on some models occasionally. Either type will do the job. The LED type of meter tends to be peak level reading while the VU is RMS (root means square) or average level. On Mackie mixers, like the one in Figure 16, the meters have a dual purpose. When a channel is set to solo, it allows the user to get a reading to set the trim pot for optimizing the input signal. This is a very handy feature in that each instrument or mike level can be set by aural and visual means.

Figure 16: Mackie 1604 Mixer Output Module and Close View of LED Meters

Headphones

Headphones are the most common devices used for listening to the different outputs from the mixer. In a noisy situation, they give the engineer a certain amount of isolation from the ambient room noise, which allows him to make critical decisions about the overall signal coming from the mixer. For instance, if the sound in the main mix speakers is distorted, you can listen to the main mix in the headphones to make sure a clean signal is leaving the mixer. If it is, then you should check the input level of the amp or the speakers themselves to see if one or all of them may be blown. A speaker is blown when its voice coil is out of round and causes a nasty sound to be produced as the cone moves back and forth. More on problems associated with P.A. systems will be discussed in the Troubleshooting section. Any output leaving the mixer can be selected by a monitor switch so that it can be heard in the headphones. Auxiliary and effect sends can be selected and their respective signals can be monitored.

Chapter Three

Amplifiers

The amplifier is the component in a P.A. system that converts the low-level output of the mixer to a usable level. The function of the amp is to increase this level high enough to drive the speaker system. As the signal exits the mixer, it enters the input of the amp and is processed through the amp's circuitry, which increases its amplitude. The amount that this level can be increased is based on the power specification of the amp.

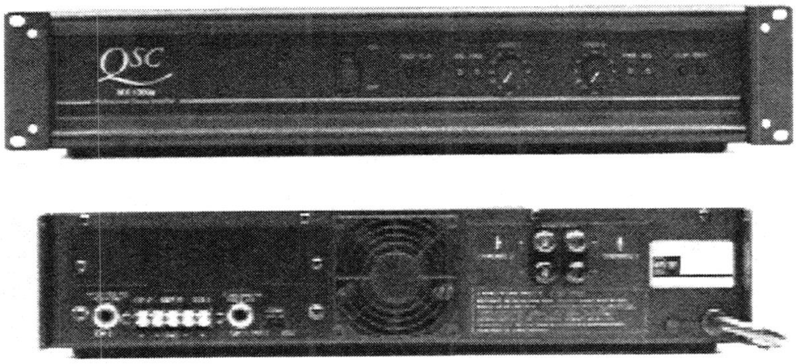

Figure 17: QSC MX1000 Power Amp, Front and Rear Views

Power Rating

This is the muscle that an amp can provide, but it can be misleading. For example, an amp delivering 250 watts of power into an 8-ohm (symbolized by the Greek letter Ω) speaker will not sound twice as loud as a 125-watt amp driving the same set of speakers. The reason for this is that our ears hear logarithmically, not linearly. That is, we hear based on ratios and not straight lines. For instance, for one amp to sound twice as loud as another, it has to deliver ten times the power! Don't worry, you don't have to buy ten amps. A common form of amplification is bi- or tri-amping. This is where an electronic crossover (a specialized P.A. component) is used to divide the different frequencies that come from the mixer into two or three different frequency sections or bands. These bands are then sent to separate amps and speakers specifically designed to handle those frequencies. I'll explain more on this subject later.

Frequency Response

Simply stated, frequency response is the range of signals, from lowest to highest frequency, that an amp can "hear" and reproduce. For example, 20 Hz to 40 kHz means the amp will respond to and reproduce signals from 20 Hz to 40 kHz.

Inputs—From Mixer

The output of the mixer is connected to the input of the power amp. The connection can be made with 1/4" phone jacks or XLR cables. You will need to check the connection types provided on the amp you plan to use. In some cases, you will need a cable that adapts an output to an input, for instance, 1/4" phone plug to XLR. The inputs can be balanced or unbalanced depending on the amp's specifications. In addition, some amps can run in stereo, two-channel mono, or bridged mono modes. This varies widely among amp models and manufacturers. Most amps have two rotary controls for setting the input sensitivity. These controls give users the ability to control the overall volume to the speakers at the amp instead of lowering the output of the mixer. By operating the mixer at optimum levels, the best signal-to-noise ratio is achieved.

Outputs—To Speakers

The speaker outputs of the amp are connected to the inputs of the speaker system. The most common connections are with 1/4" phone jacks. Many amps, however, have binding posts or banana plugs as optional output connections. The 1/4" phone's positive locking feature (it clicks into place) or the screw-down mechanism of the binding posts provide the most secure connections from the amp.

Chapter Four

Loudspeakers

Loudspeakers are transducers (devices that transmit energy from one system to another) that convert voltage to sound. (Mikes and guitar pickups are also transducers, but they work in reverse—converting sound to voltage.) This conversion is done by the speaker's cone movement. When an amp sends voltage to a speaker, it is analogous to, or the same as, the original sound waveform that comes from the mike or instrument. As this voltage causes the speaker coil to move back and forth around the speaker's magnet, sound pressure is created in the air by the speaker cone. This is the sound pressure level (SPL). The difference between the original sound and the sound from the speakers is that the speaker sound is louder. That's why we use the phrase "to amplify the sound."

There are two types of speakers used in a P.A. system: mains and monitors. The mains deliver the sound to the audience while the stage monitors keep the band synchronized. Main speakers can be a single cabinet housing a number of different components to cover the frequency range. Three common components are the woofer, the horn, and the tweeter. The woofer is the low- and mid-range driver and can be an 18", 15", or 12" speaker. A radial horn may be included, which is a mid-range driver attached to a fiberglass horn that disperses the sound in a wide directed range. And the tweeter is a small diaphragm speaker that is designed to deliver high frequencies. These are all connected with an internal crossover to protect each driver from receiving potentially damaging frequencies. The large sound reinforcement systems employ this same principal but use separate cabinets loaded with one type of speaker to cover a narrow frequency range. In a large set-up, you might have a sub-woofer cabinet with an 18" speaker for the very low frequencies, a low-frequency cabinet loaded with 15" speakers, a mid-range cabinet with 12" speakers or radial horn, and a high-frequency array that may have horns and/or tweeters.

Figure 18: JBL Full-Range Speaker Systems

Stage monitors function pretty much the same as the mains, but they differ in size, shape, and frequency response. Sometimes referred to as wedges because of their shape, they are designed to be placed on the floor of the stage facing the performer(s), not the audience. A separate mix is sent to an amp from the mixer to power these speakers. Sometimes a volume control is on the speaker, so each musician is in control of the sound level. In other cases, a built-in amplifier can be placed in the cabinet to eliminate the need for external power amps. These cabinets are usually used by vocalists to hear themselves and to keep the band in sync. Since they are not designed to be as full range as the main speakers, their sound quality is not as high.

Figure 19: JBL and Fender Stage Monitor Speakers

Impedance

A speaker's impedance is rated in ohms (Ω). Impedance is the amount of resistance a speaker provides to the amp's electrical current. By knowing the impedance of your speakers, you can match them properly to the amplifier. In order for an amp to deliver a specified amount of power, it has to be connected to a known resistance. Care has to be taken when connecting more than one set of speakers to a power amp. The reason is that there are two types of connections available: series and parallel. When two sets of speakers of the same impedance are connected in series, the impedance is doubled; for example, two 8Ω speakers will combine to offer 16Ω of resistance. In a parallel connection, the same 8Ω speakers will halve to offer only 4Ω of resistance. As you can see in Figure 20, this can dramatically change what the amp sees for impedance.

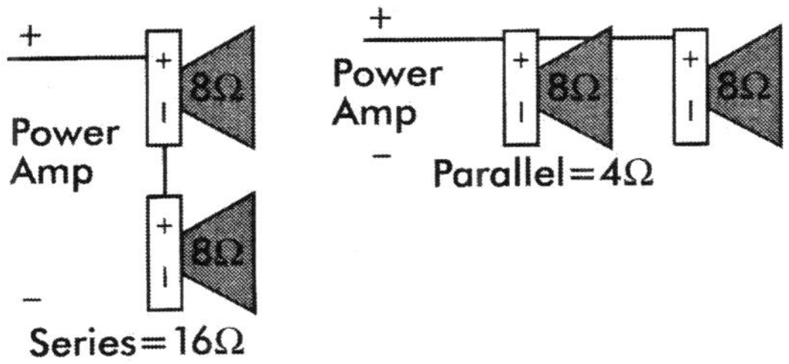

Figure 20: Series and Parallel Connections

Frequency Response

As in the power amp, frequency response is the spectrum of sounds from lowest to highest that the speakers can "hear" and then reproduce. What I mean by speakers "hearing" is that they respond to voltage that comes from the amplifier. This amp voltage carries all of the original frequencies that come from the mixer and are amplified many times over. The speakers must respond to this amplified signal to send the sound of the original sounds to the audience. Think of the difference when listening to your favorite CD on a boom box or a home stereo system. Big difference, right? That's because the more sophisticated home stereo has speakers with better frequency response. Most of them have large, medium, and small coned speakers in the cabinet. The large cone moves more air and responds primarily to the lower frequency spectrum, the medium cone responds to the midrange frequencies, and the small cone responds to the higher sounds. Modern P.A. systems use this same type of technology to reproduce sounds throughout the frequency range. This description of how speakers respond to different frequencies is simplified, but it should give you a basic understanding of how speakers respond to incoming signals.

Power Ratings

Many years ago, I worked as a stereo equipment salesman. During slow times, my coworkers and I would engage in a pastime we called "blow up the car stereo speakers." We used speakers that had been returned because of defects. We took an old electrical extension cord and stripped the wire so it could be connected to the speaker leads. When the cord was plugged into an electrical outlet, the speakers exploded. Looking back, I realize that this was dangerous and stupid since there was danger from both the electrical outlet and the violent explosion of the speakers. I'm telling you this only as a graphic example of what power ratings are all about: Deliver too much power to a speaker system and it will blow up! A speaker is designed to reproduce specific frequencies when a certain amount of power is applied. How much power a speaker can handle has to do with the size of the magnet, the number of wraps in the coil around the cone, and the frequencies coming in from the amp. A speaker's power rating is expressed in sound pressure levels (SPL), which are expressed in decibels (dB) that will be at a specified distance when a certain amount of power is applied. For example, a speaker can produce 96 dB SPL at 1 meter at 1 watt. A very small speaker will distort even with little power applied if it is fed very low sounds. This is because the coil will travel up and down the magnet but will be driven so far that it will slap or jam on the extreme travel ranges. Remember that the higher the SPL rating, the more efficient the speakers.

Speaker Placement

When setting up a sound system, the main house speakers should be placed in front of the band, never behind it, to avoid feedback. If speakers are placed behind a microphone, the sound coming into that mike is sent to the speakers and then the sound from those same speakers re-enters the mike. This cycle continues until a feedback loop is created in the system and a high-pitched howling sound is generated through the P.A. Other considerations and questions are:

Should the speakers be elevated?
How close to an adjacent wall should they be placed?
Is the room very live (like a high school gym)?

All of these factors have a definite effect on how the overall speaker system will sound, which frequencies will be reinforced and boosted, and which frequencies will be canceled out. There is no such thing as a perfect room, so a P.A. equalizer (EQ) can balance the frequency spectrum to reproduce more uniform sound. We'll cover more on EQ in the Signal Processing section.

Speaker Wire Gauges

Speaker wire gauges are to current flow as garden and fire hoses are to water flow. Would you want to fill up an in-ground swimming pool using a garden hose? No! Simply put, all speaker cables have a certain amount of electrical resistance and essentially eat some of the power from your amp before it gets to the speakers. As far as wire gauges are concerned, less is more for two reasons. First, the smaller the gauge number, the larger the cable because there are more strands of wire in it. Second, the smaller the gauge number, the less electrical resistance, so 12- and 10-gauge wire are the best choices.

Another consideration for speaker wire is that you do not want to use a shielded cable, similar to a guitar cord, for connecting the speakers to the amp. A guitar cable has a single connection inside a plastic tube to carry the hot (positive) signal. The shield is then braided around the plastic tube and is connected to the ground post. The problem with using this type of cable to connect the speakers to the amp is that amplifier power generates heat in the cable. If the shield melts through the plastic tube, the cables will be exposed to each other, short out the system, and may possibly blow up the power amp. This usually won't happen in one night, but over time the constant heat may degrade the cable and cause the short. Use only high-quality cables designed to do specific jobs, and you will probably never have a problem due to cable failures.

Another problem to avoid is the short circuit. A short circuit occurs when there is a direct path between the two polarities of the output of an amp. If the positive and negative speaker wires are connected together, the amp sees no resistance! Then the amp tries to deliver power that exceeds its power rating and either goes into thermal overload and shuts down or blows up. Be sure to keep negative and positive wires separate.

Chapter Five

Signal Processing

A signal processor is a component that either modifies the original input signal and then blends it back with the original or sends the modified signal to the outputs of the mixer. Reverbs and digital delays are typical devices that are blended with the original signal. A graphic equalizer modifies the tonal characteristics of a sound. In this case, the original signal is not remixed with the processed sound since the purpose of using a graphic EQ is to enhance certain frequency bands.

Types of Processors

Reverb

What exactly is reverb (short for *reverberation*)? We use the term a lot and refer to the sound as being "wet." How reverberant a room is depends on size; building materials; shape; and absorbing materials like chairs, tables, and people. Clubs, churches, gyms, and concert halls all have a certain amount of reverb time, some more or less than others. Reverb is an electrical unit, like the one in Figure 21, used to replicate the acoustical environment found in those types of places.

A sound in a room travels in all directions, hits walls and floors, loses a certain amount of energy, and then reflects again and again off of these surfaces until it is below audible levels. This mixes with the original sound and creates a delay that is perceptible to our hearing. Reverb time is the name for the number of reflections and the length of time it takes for them to die out. Churches and large halls with high ceilings have longer reverb times than dance clubs with low ceilings. In addition, certain frequencies are reinforced in some situations, for example, the bass sounds in a gym. I'm sure you are familiar with the booming sound that seems to fill a gym. It is a big low-frequency standing wave that bounces off all four cement walls and hardwood basketball floor and really does fill the room.

If you use a long reverb time effect, you'll get the sensation you're in a church or hall. This could be weird if you're playing in a small club because you don't get the perception of a large space from anything else around you. A real dead sounding room cries for some reverb to add a little life to the sound.

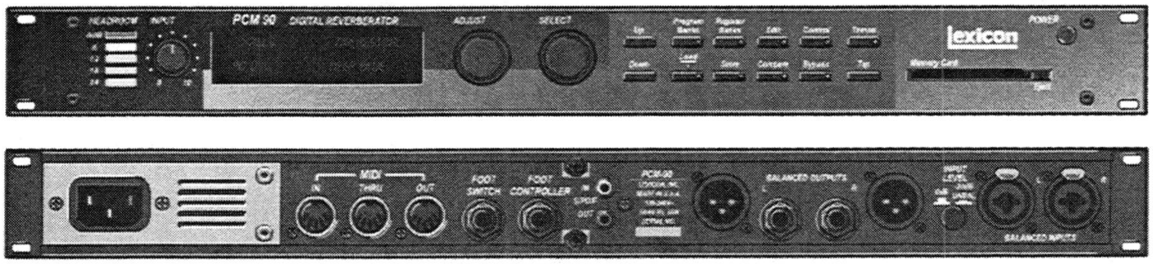

Figure 21: Lexicon PCM 90 Digital Reverb
Front Panel and Rear Connections

Digital Delays

This is probably one of the most used signal processors and the easiest to understand. Digital delay is used by both vocalists and instrumentalists to produce that slap back echo sound that just about everyone uses with a little reverb. What does a digital delay do? It takes the original input signal and processes it through a series of circuits. During this process, the signal's time is held back or delayed (from milliseconds to a few seconds) and then sent to the output. This delayed signal may or may not be mixed with the original depending on the desired effect. If the original signal is not mixed with the delayed signal, the only thing you will hear is the delayed sound. This obviously is not a good thing since it sounds like the singer is not in time with the rest of the band! Most digital delays can create effects such as chorus, slap back echo, or even delays of three seconds or more. Each effect is created by setting specific controls on the unit to different delay times, feedback, and mix. Most units have pages you can scroll through to set specific parameters, but these controls can be more easily understood if you look at older units that use plain rotary pots.

The main controls on a digital delay are input, delay, feedback, and mix. The input control adjusts the level coming into the unit. This is associated with the level meter on the front panel. The input control should be adjusted while a signal is applied to the input by either singing into a mike or playing an instrument. The pot is rotated clockwise until the meter reads 0 VU. Take care not to overload the unit by peaking into the red on the meters. The next control is the delay time, usually shown in milliseconds. For example, one thousand milliseconds (1000 ms) equals one second. The math is really easy. The decimal point is always at the end of the number. By moving it three places to the left, you get the amount of delay time in seconds. For instance, 1200 ms is 1.2 seconds, and 3400 ms is 3.4 seconds. The feedback control allows the user to delay the delayed signal. By increasing this pot, the delayed signal is fed back into the input mixed with the delayed signal and fed into the input again. The higher the control setting, the more pronounced the repeating effect becomes. Finally, the mix pot sets the proportion of original signal and delayed signal at the output of the device. Depending on the desired effect, this control is usually set to let more original signals pass with a lesser amount of delay.

Equalizers

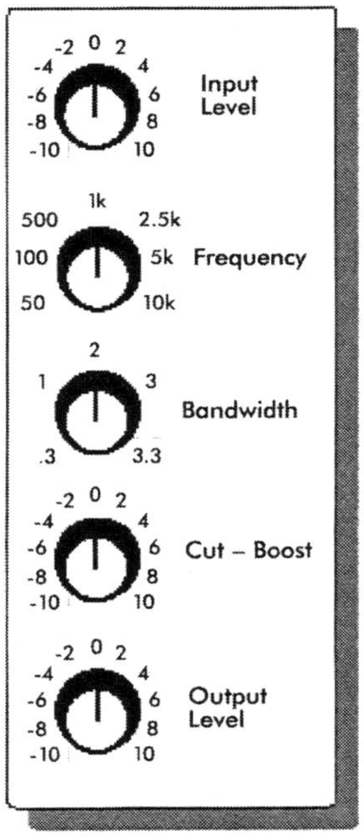

Figure 22: Parametric EQ

There are two types of equalizers commonly used in a P.A. system, parametric and graphic. Each functions in a very specific way, so they are used for different applications.

The parametric EQ is a unit that can be used to dial-in on very narrow bands in the frequency spectrum to enhance a deficient sound or cut out an unwanted frequency. The controls on the parametric EQ are input level, boost and cut, frequency, bandwidth (Q), and output. The input level controls the amplitude of the signal entering the unit and should be set as high as possible without overloading the unit. The frequency control allows the user to dial-in the frequency to be adjusted. The bandwidth, or Q, controls how wide or narrow the adjustment. The bandwidth can be set anywhere from 1/3 of an octave to 3 octaves. This allows for adjustments ranging from very fine to very broad when boost or cut is applied to the signal. The output controls the signal level leaving the unit and should be adjusted to the same level as the unprocessed signal entering the unit's input.

Graphic equalizers are usually connected between the mixer and power amp and are used to adjust the overall frequency response of the room. The graphic EQ has a number of sliders on the front panel. There can be as few as seven or as many as 31. The number of sliders reflects how accurately you can work in a specific frequency range, although they do overlap to some extent. The sliders have a center indent that is labeled 0 dB. In this position, no EQ is applied to any of the frequencies. A certain amount of boost or cut is available and can be any range, but 12–18 dB is common. As each of the bands is adjusted, the sliders form a graphic chart of the EQ being applied to the signal, giving this unit its name.

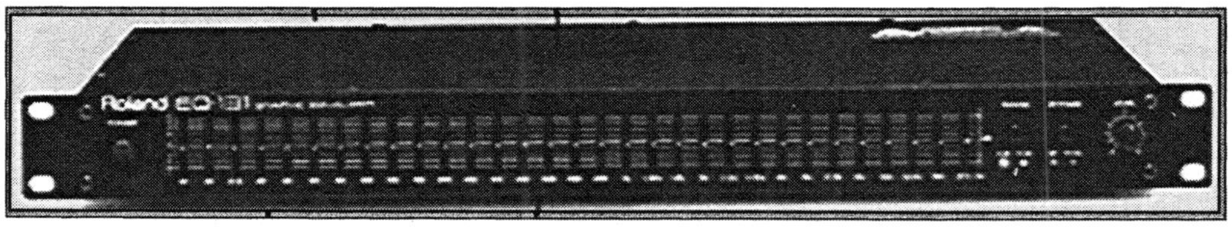

Figure 23: Roland 31 Band Monophonic Graphic EQ

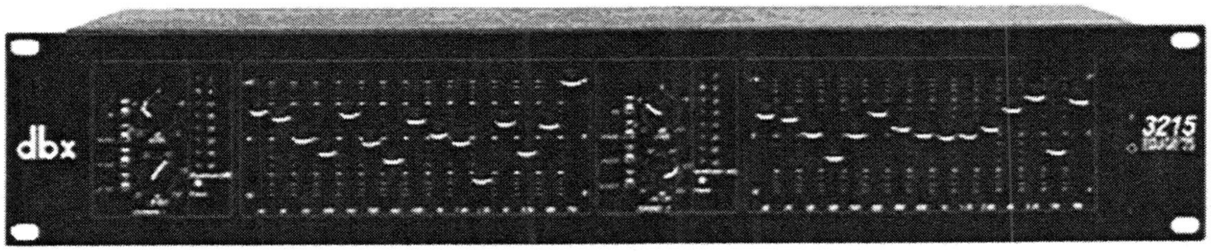

Figure 24: DBX 15-Band Stereo Graphic EQ

Compressors

A compressor is a signal processor that acts as a very fast gain control. This unit is used to set a level. If that level is exceeded, the unit will automatically reduce the gain at its output. The main controls on a compressor are threshold, ratio, attack, release, and output. The threshold control is expressed in decibels and is used to set the specified level that you want to maintain. At 0 dB, the unit is set to reduce the gain only on signals that are above the 0-dB level at the unit's input. The ratio pot controls the amount of gain reduction after the threshold level is exceeded. For example, if you set the ratio pot to 2:1, the compressor will reduce the gain 2 dB for every 1 dB above the threshold setting. At ∞:1 (∞=infinity), the compressor becomes a limiter and will not allow any signal to cross the 0-dB mark. The attack pot controls how fast the compressor will react to incoming signals. The release controls how fast it will let go to react to the attack setting. When you set the attack and release controls to their minimum (fastest reaction) settings and input a signal consistently over the threshold, a pumping and breathing effect will occur. This is because the compressor acts on the signal immediately by releasing the signal and then acting on it again. This effect can be reduced dramatically by increasing the attack time slightly and making the release time longer. The output pot controls the volume exiting the compressor and should be set to the approximate level of the signal entering the input before the threshold is exceeded.

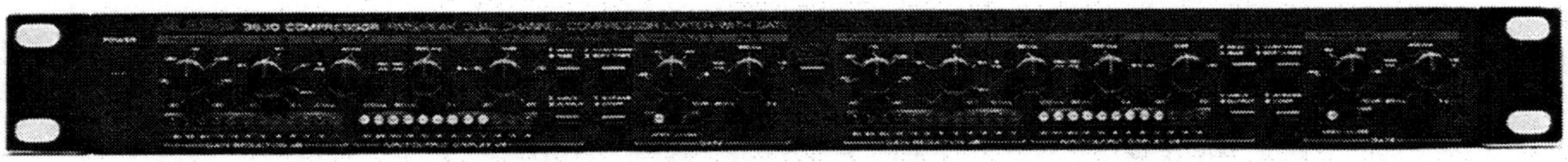

Figure 25: Alesis 3030 Compressor/Noise Gate

Figure 26: DBX 160A Compressor/Limiter

Noise Gates

Sometimes it is easier to think of one device as the reverse of another. This may be so in the case of a noise gate, also called a gate or an expander. A noise gate acts in a manner that is the reverse of a compressor. In other words, if a compressor reduces gain on a signal that exceeds the threshold setting, then a noise gate permits a signal at an appropriate threshold level to pass. This device, when used properly, can be used effectively to control almost any mike on stage, from the vocalist's to the snare drum's. Guitarists use noise gates the most. Guitar pickups generate noise by picking up signals from lighting and interference. This noise is below the playing level of the guitar and is masked by the guitar sound once the musician is playing. By setting the threshold low enough, the noise gate will impede the signal flow and cut out unwanted sounds. So the guitar signal will be silent until a note is struck on the instrument. At that point the gate will open and the guitar signal will pass through the unit's circuitry. If the threshold is set too high, even the guitar signal won't open the gate, so this setting is crucial to proper operation. The other control on the gate is the release or rate pot that controls how quickly the gate will close. If you set the time too short, the signal will be cut too soon. If you set the time too long, the noise will be present even after the instrument signal is gone.

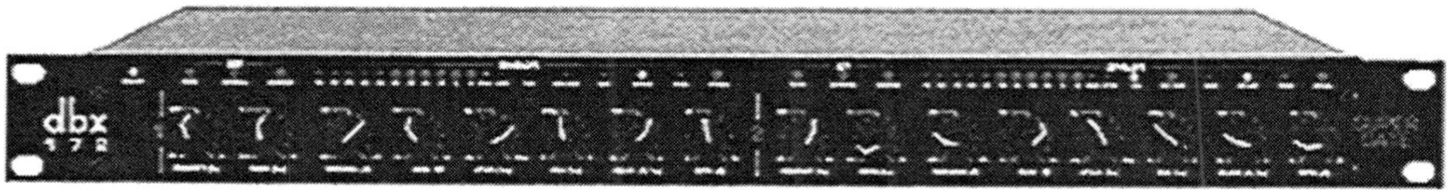

Figure 27: DBX SuperGate Noise Gate

Multi-Effects Processors

This device is one in which a number of signal processors are built into a single unit. It is not uncommon for a multi-effects processor, like the one in Figure 28, to have a reverb, a delay, a chorus, a compressor, a noise gate, and an equalizer. Each individual processor is selected and then parameters are set. The final chain of processing events can be saved as a patch and called up instantaneously from the front panel. This is very handy if you perform in the same club on a regular basis. Set the patch the first time you perform and recall it every time to play in that club.

Figure 28: Alesis QuadraVerb4 Multi-Effects Processor

Electronic Crossovers

Although it's not really a signal processor like the ones mentioned on the previous pages, this particular device is used in many multi-amp/multi-speaker sound systems. It is used for bi- or tri-amplification of a speaker system. The mixer feeds the crossover with a broadband of frequencies, and the crossover divides this broadband into two or more narrower bands. Since speakers are designed with specific frequency response ratings, the crossover outputs are connected to the appropriate amps and speakers in the array. By using a crossover and bi- or tri-amplification, a system amplifier's power is used efficiently, and the speakers are protected from potentially damaging frequencies.

One of the most important aspects of the electronic crossover is that it permits the user to select the frequencies' crossover point. This allows for a variety of speakers to be used since the selectable frequencies on the crossover can be set to meet the required specifications.

Figure 29: DBX 234 Electronic Crossover

Connecting to the Mixer

When you are ready to connect outboard processing to the mixer, you must consider what you will send to the equipment. Then you will decide to use either an aux send or channel or main mix inserts. Reverbs, for instance, are almost always connected to the aux sends since you will want to vary the amount of reverb applied to each channel. A vocal mike will require more reverb than a bass guitar or kick drum mike. Varying the amount of reverb applied to each channel creates a pleasing effect and a realistic room environment. The same would hold true for a digital delay.

Graphic equalizers and compressors, on the other hand, are normally connected to the main mix channel inserts. In this way, the entire mix is processed by these devices to accomplish a sonic quality or controlled volume level in the room. Not all mixers have channel inserts. If your mixer doesn't have channel inserts, then the main mix out should be connected to the input of the EQ, and the EQ output should be connected to the input of the power amp.

There are also considerations with regard to the sequence in which outboard devices are connected. You might be wondering, "Should the EQ come before the compressor or the compressor before the EQ?" The answer to both is "yes" depending on the desired outcome and performance of the system. I'll discuss these issues in more detail in the Making the Connections section.

Aux Sends

The auxiliary send section on a mixer consists of a channel send pot, a main aux send pot, an output jack, stereo pair return input jacks, and a return volume pot. Here's the way they work together. Let's say we want to apply some reverb to a singer's voice whose mike is plugged into channel 1 on the mixer. There are three parts to this process.

The first thing to do is make the connection to the reverb unit. Consider the following: Does the reverb unit have stereo inputs? Do both channels have to be driven or can you feed a mono signal into a single channel? The aux send output will usually be mono, so if you need to drive both channels of the stereo reverb unit, you will need a Y cable to come from the mixer out. (See Figure 30.) If you can drive a single channel (usually marked "mono") of the reverb unit, connect the mixer out to the reverb in with the appropriate cable. Most mixers have stereo aux returns to accommodate signal processing outputs. Here you connect the reverb unit out to the aux returns in. (See Figure 31.)

The second thing to do is to set the reverb's mix control to send only reverb sound back to the mixer. The reason for this is to mix a certain amount of the original dry signal with a balanced amount of reverb using the aux returns.

The third thing to do is to set the aux sends to drive the reverb unit's input at an optimum level to achieve the best signal-to-noise ratio. Most reverb units have a built-in metering system. You need to drive the unit at a level high enough to process signals but low enough so that it doesn't overdrive the unit's input. Set the main aux send out to the 12 o'clock position (usually halfway up). Then, while singing into the mike, gradually bring up the channel aux send until the meters on the reverb unit flash in the green and occasionally peak into the yellow. Red lights indicate that you are clipping (overdriving) the reverb's inputs. Finally, bring up the aux returns until the amount of reverb you want is introduced into the main mix.

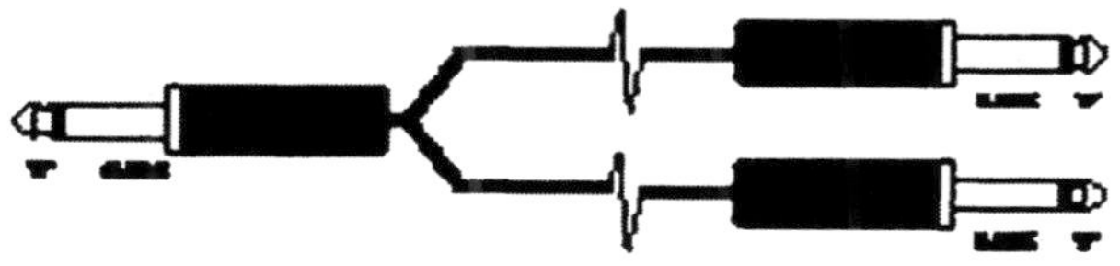

Figure 30: 1/4" TS to (2) 1/4" TS phone plug Y cable

Figure 31: Main Aux Send and Returns on a Mackie 1604 VLZ Mixer

Inserts

These jacks on the mixer are actually send and receive. The cable used for this connection is a tip/ring/sleeve (TRS) 1/4" phone plug connected to two 1/4" tip/sleeve (TS) phone plugs. The tip on the TRS plug sends the signal to the tip of one of the 1/4" TS phones (the send) and the ring is connected to the tip of the other (the return). The sleeves are all connected to the shield as a common ground. This creates a path for the signal to be sent from the mixer to the input of, say, an equalizer. The output of the EQ is returned to the mixer. Since the signal is interrupted in the mixer internally when a cable is plugged into the insert jack, no signal will pass unless the outboard equipment is connected properly. That means you won't get any signal out of the mixer, so you won't have sound coming out of the P.A.! Many times I've seen musicians scratching their heads trying to troubleshoot a P.A. only to find out that one of the plugs connected to an insert was not seated all the way.

A common use of channel inserts is to connect a graphic equalizer to the mixer in order to modify the frequency response of a room. Unlike the aux sends, you don't mix the original and processed signals; instead, you process the signal to change it completely. Here are the connections for using this device and the main mix insert jacks.

1. Connect the TRS 1/4" plug to the main mix left insert jack.
2. Connect the send 1/4" TS plug to the input of the graphic EQ. This plug usually has a red casing or red strip on it.
3. Connect the other 1/4" TS to the output of the graphic EQ. This plug will probably have a black casing or strip.
4. Make sure the input control on the EQ is about halfway up, and then sing or play an instrument into the mixer. You should now see levels entering the graphic EQ on its input metering system. If the level is too low, gradually increase the input control on the EQ until the levels are within the proper operating range.
5. Repeat the above procedure with the right insert jack.

Chapter Six

Microphones

A microphone is a transducer that converts sound into an electrical voltage (signal). The microphone's characteristics are determined by the type of mike and its polar pattern or patterns. A microphone's type can be dynamic (a moving coil or ribbon), condenser (also known as a capacitor mike), or electret condenser. The polar pattern of a mike is a graph that shows its frequency response at different angles as sound hits the diaphragm. A mike with good frequency rejection off-axis (from behind or off to the side of the mike) is useful in eliminating feedback sometimes produced by stage monitor systems. Microphone polar patterns fall into two categories. The omni-directional mike is equally sensitive to frequencies from all directions. The uni-directional mike is most sensitive to sound frequencies directly approaching the front of it (on-axis).

When you purchase a microphone, it will almost always come with a mike clip or holder to mount it on a stand. Always keep the clip with the mike; do not leave it on the stand. One reason is that the clip may break in transit on the mike stand. Clips are made of high-impact plastic, but throwing them in the back of a truck on the stand is just asking for trouble. Another reason is that not all mikes have the same barrel, so they won't interchange easily and may break if a large mike is squeezed into a small clip. Another tip: When mounting a mike clip on a stand, loosen the clutch on the stand pole and hold the mike clip over the threading on the stand. Turn the stand pole clockwise (not the mike and not the entire stand) to tighten the clip on the stand, and then adjust the height of the stand and tighten the clutch. You'll be amazed how much easier this is rather than turning the mike clip. To take the clip off the stand, just reverse the procedure.

Types of Microphones

Dynamic

Dynamic mikes usually fall into two categories, moving coil and ribbon, as seen in Figure 32. In a moving coil mike, a diaphragm is attached to a coil of thin wire. When sound pressure causes the diaphragm to move, it passes the coil around a fixed magnet. As you may remember from science class, this generates voltage at the output, which can then be amplified by the mike pre-amp of the mixer. A ribbon mike uses a metal ribbon suspended in a magnet. When sound pressure causes the ribbon to move in the magnetic field, voltage is generated at the mike's output. Ribbon mikes are almost always bi-directional because of the way the ribbon is suspended in the magnet. Sound approaching from the side can't create much motion in the ribbon, so little voltage is generated.

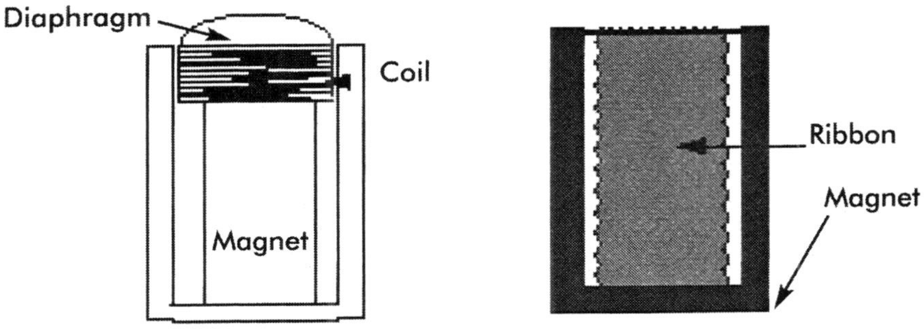

Figure 32: Moving Coil Mike Capsule and Ribbon Mike Capsule

Condenser (Phantom Power)

A condenser or capacitor mike uses an electrically charged flexible diaphragm and a hard plate charged with an opposite polarity. When the diaphragm moves, a small charge is generated and is amplified by an internal transformer in the mike itself. A condenser mike always requires an outside source of electricity to power it. The most common form of power is called phantom power and is provided by the mixer. Many modern mixers have a phantom power switch that delivers the voltage to both the positive and negative leads on the mike cable (one to the mike's diaphragm and the other to the plate). Since both lines get exactly the same voltage, but of opposite polarity, the mixer's mike input cannot see this polarizing voltage at the mike's output. That's where the term *phantom power* comes from.

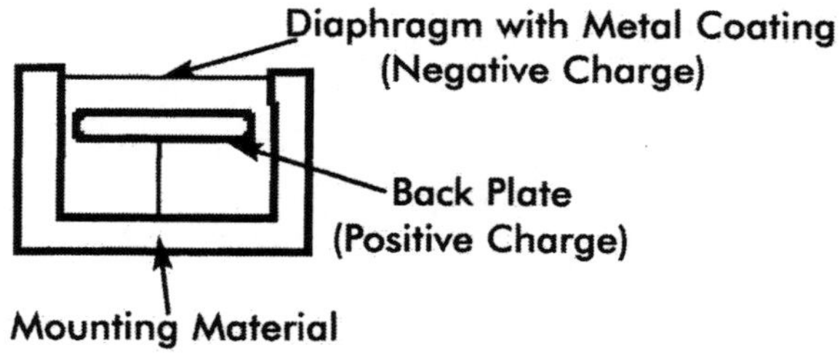

Figure 33: Condenser Mike capsule

Electret Condenser (Battery)

An electret condenser mike is very similar to a condenser mike. The big difference is that the plate and diaphragm are charged at the factory and the power is usually provided by a single AA battery. Over time, the plates have a tendency to lose their charge, resulting in a lower voltage (loss of power) at the mike's output. This mike, however, is much less costly than a condenser mike that uses phantom power.

Polar Patterns

A microphone's polar pattern is a graph of the sensitivity to frequencies coming from a full 360°. The front of the mike at the capsule is 0° and 360° on-axis; the back of the mike is 180° off-axis; and the left and right sides are 90° off-axis. Picture a mike on a stand in the center of a circular track. On the track is a speaker that can travel completely around the microphone. As the speaker moves around the mike and plays different frequencies (low to high), we can plot the microphone's sensitivity to selected sounds from different angles. This gives us very valuable information as to the frequency response of the microphone and where, if any, the greatest rejection of sound (the points where the mike can't hear) occurs.

Remember that the range of human hearing covers 20,000 cycles. It wouldn't make sense to plot every frequency because it would look like a big black blotch. Instead, selected frequencies are plotted to give an overall view of the frequency response. Sometimes two graphs are used to divide the frequency ranges to make them more readable.

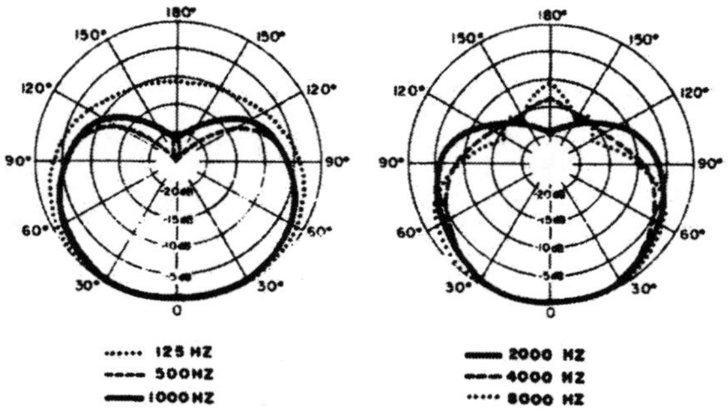

Figure 34: A Typical Microphone Polar Pattern Graph

Omni-Directional

Omni-directional means "all directions." This type of polar pattern depicts a mike that is sensitive equally to frequencies coming from the front, sides, and back of it. Although it is good for many recording situations, this type of mike is not very practical in live sound situations. It is too susceptible to feedback since it will receive sound from just about any direction, including that of the main speakers and monitor system.

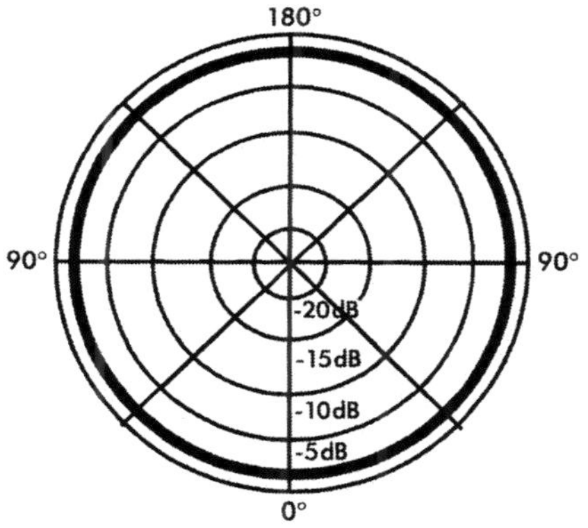

Figure 35: Omni Polar Pattern

Uni-Directional

A uni-directional mike is more sensitive to frequencies coming directly into the front of it (on-axis). Since this type of mike is less sensitive to sounds coming from the sides or back, it is widely used in sound reinforcement.

Cardioid

This type of uni-directional mike gets its name from its heart-shaped polar pattern. The greatest rejection is directly off-axis (the back of the mike) or 180°. Since this is where stage monitors are usually placed, this type of mike is a top choice for live sound applications.

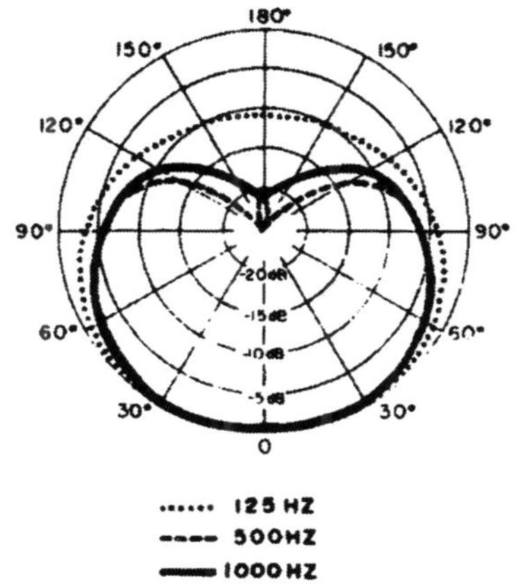

Figure 36: Uni-Directional Cardioid Polar Pattern

Bi-Directional

As I pointed out, ribbon mikes, based on the way they work, have a bi-directional polar pattern. This is because the mike is equally sensitive on each side of the ribbon. The greatest rejection is not 180° off-axis but at the 90° and 270° points. This mike is not used too often in sound reinforcement because it is just as sensitive at the back as in the front. Stage monitors would cause this mike to produce feedback, and audience sound would be amplified into the P.A. Ribbon bi-directional mikes are usually used in recording studios and other specialized recording situations. The bi-directional pattern is sometimes referred to as a figure 8 pattern because of the way the graph looks.

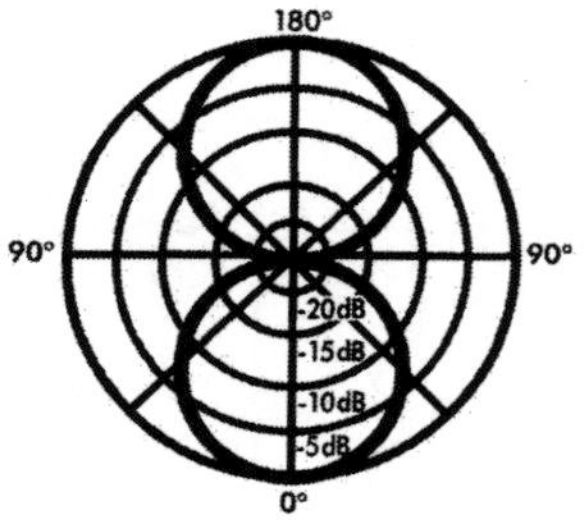

Figure 37: Figure 8 Bi-Directional Polar Pattern

Impedance

Microphones come in both high and low impedance. Most mikes used professionally are low impedance since, when used with a balanced XLR cable, they offer the greatest noise rejection and offer long cable runs. Low-impedance mikes are 600 ohms and are plugged into the mike inputs of the mixer with an XLR connector. High-impedance mikes usually come with a cable that has a 1/4-inch phone plug connector and is 25 feet long or less.

Wireless Systems

Wireless mike and guitar systems have become popular because of the freedom of movement they offer the performer and because they provide an almost cable-free stage floor. They are, however, not without their shortcomings. Interference and price are the two main issues concerning this type of system. There are two types of systems available: ultra-high frequency (UHF) and very high frequency (VHF). Both of these systems are available with dual antennae and receivers. A system that uses a microprocessor to monitor the two incoming signals and uses the strongest one to send to its output is known as a diversity system. The two main parts of a wireless system are the transmitter and the receiver. The transmitter for a standard hand-held microphone plugs directly into the mike's XLR output. On guitar systems and small mikes used for saxophones or other wind instruments, there is a small transmitter that is usually worn on the performer's belt. The mike or guitar is then plugged into the transmitter, which in turn sends the signal to the receiver. The output of the receiver is plugged into the input of the mixer or guitar amp.

UHF

This system is considered the flagship of the two systems and is the more expensive. The advantage is that the UHF frequency range is uncluttered and many channels are available. The disadvantage is that UHF signals are not very large, so obstructions can cause problems.

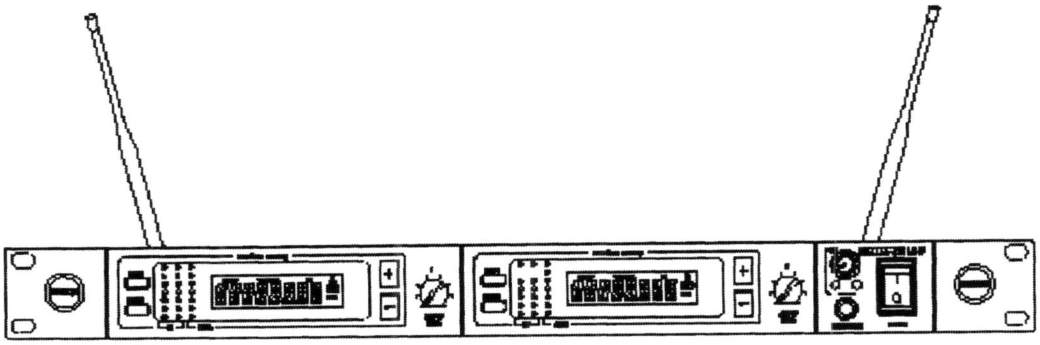

Figure 38: UHF Receiver

VHF

This system is widely used since the price is more affordable than the UHF system. The main disadvantage here is that there are less channels available due in part to its popular use among many bands. This system produces a much larger transmission wave, which is less susceptible to obstructions, so problems associated with drop-outs are less likely.

Cables, Snakes, and the Gig Toolbox

I've already covered most of the cables used for connections of a P.A. system, but I think a section with all of them for quick reference is a good idea. This section is also a good spot to bring up cable snakes. The cable snake that is used in an audio system is a multi-connector box that can have female 1/4" phone jacks and/or XLR connections on one end and 1/4" phone plugs and XLR connectors on the other. Snakes can be 25, 50, or 100 or more feet in length. The longer snakes usually have only XLR low-impedance connections. These are friends of the P.A. sound reinforcement engineer because they allow cable to be run to the main mixer, which can be located somewhere out in the audience area. Obviously, the best place to run a P.A. is where you hear the same sound as the audience. Without cable snakes, the amount of wire running to the back of the room would be impossible to manage. With them, the connector box is placed on stage and the mikes and instruments are plugged into them. The opposite end of the snake allows the appropriate connections to be made to the mixer. The snake also has returns that run from the mixer back to the stage, which allow for the mixer's outputs to be sent back to the stage area where they can be connected to the main and stage monitor power amps. Even if you run your P.A. from the stage, a snake can keep the stage tidy and free from stretched or dangerously run cables in many circumstances.

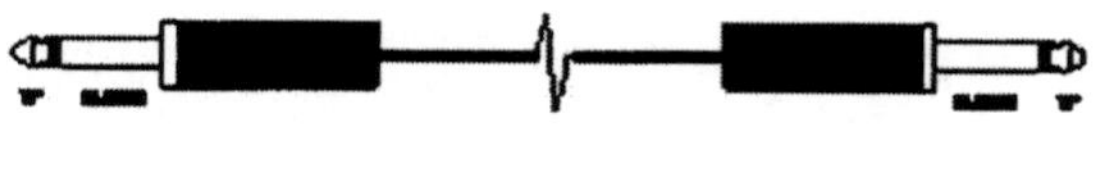

1/4" Tip/Sleeve (TS) Unbalanced

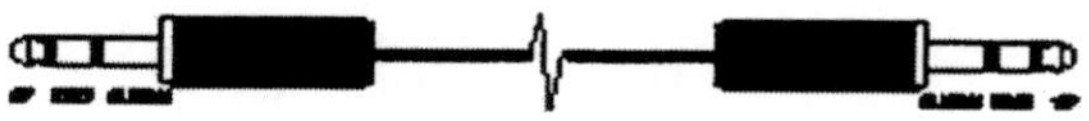

1/4" Tip/Ring/Sleeve (TRS) Balanced

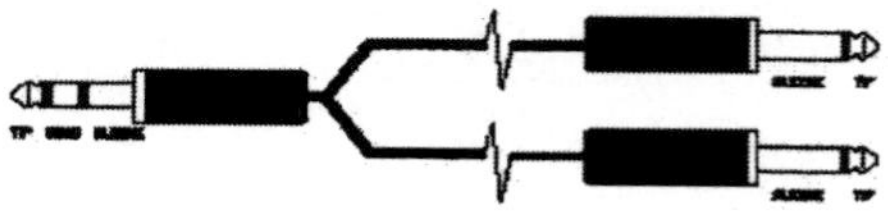

1/4" Y Tip/Ring/Sleeve to (2) Tip/Sleeve (TS) for Inserts

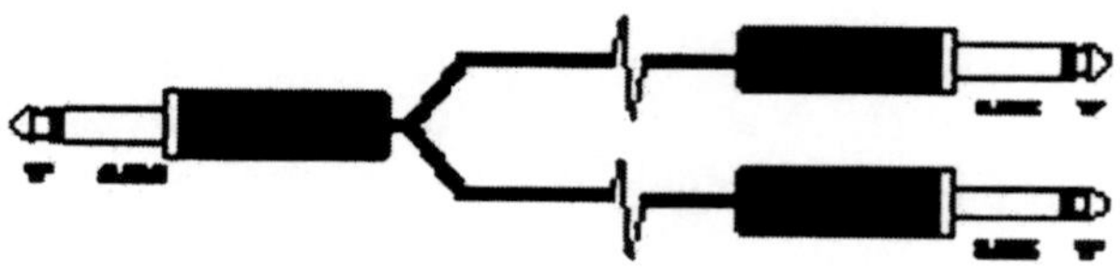

1/4" TS to (2) 1/4" TS Phone Plug Y Cable

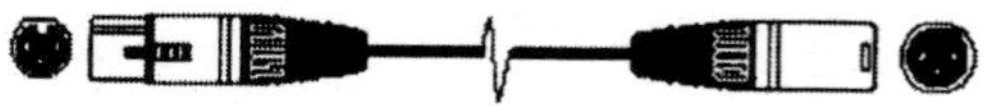

XLR Balanced

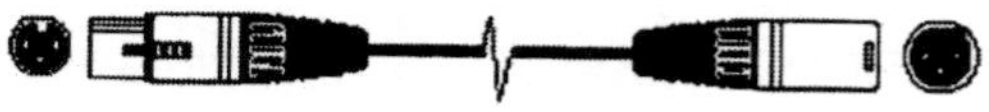

XLR Unbalanced

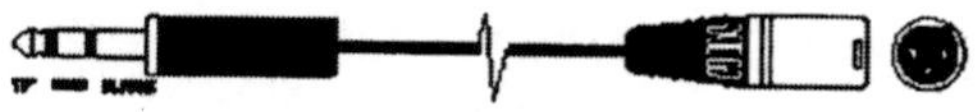

1/4" Tip/Ring/Sleeve (TRS) to XLR Balanced

Figure 39: Various Cable Types

What is a Gig Toolbox? It's a bag with essential items that can help bail you out of some bad situations. The following is a list of items you should carry and how they can be used. I don't leave the house without them.

Duct tape
This stuff is probably used more by musicians than air conditioning and ventilation professionals. The most common use is to tape cables down to the floor or to make Xs to mark the locations of the band musicians. You can do almost anything with duct tape. I once forgot my guitar strap, so I made one out of duct tape by folding a long piece in half, cutting holes where the guitar pegs would go through, and then trimming off the excess.

AC circuit tester
This is a Radio Shack item (cat. #22-101) that I carry around. It lets me know that the cables in the wall are connected properly. It has three lights that represent six different conditions that can exist in the wiring of a three-pronged electrical outlet. They are: open ground, open neutral, open hot, hot and ground reversed, hot and neutral reversed, and correct connections. Since every piece of electrical equipment will be connected to the electrical outlets, it's important to know all is well on the other side of the wall.

Multitester
This is not absolutely necessary, but it does help troubleshoot a number of problems. First of all, you can test that the electricity coming from the wall is 117 volts. I've seen more equipment damaged by low voltage rather then by high-powered spikes. Since these units can also measure resistance, they can be used to check cable continuity when a dedicated cable tester is not available. Finally, you can check to see if your speakers are at their rated impedance.

AC extension cables and power strips

Phillips and flat-head screwdrivers (medium and small)

Flashlight

Utility razor or carpet knife

Marker pen

1/4" paper tape
Used in identifying channel connections on the console.

Soldering gun and solder

Assorted adapters

Properly rated fuses for the amps, mixers, etc.

Three-pronged to two-pronged grounded AC adapters

I'm sure you will think of additional items to carry with you. If you use something to repair, connect, write, solder, or tape anything in your P.A., carry it with you. If you don't, you will need it when something in the system fails.

Chapter Seven

Making the Connections

A sound system is chained together by connecting the output of one component to the input of another. There is a specific order that must be followed to make the system work. In the most basic set-up, this is the way it is done:

1. The output of the mike or musical instrument is connected to the input channel of the mixer.
2. The main mix output of the mixer is connected to the input of the amplifier.
3. The speaker output of the amp is connected to the input of the speakers.

This is a very simple set-up, so let's explore a more sophisticated system with stage monitors and signal processors.

Multiple Instruments and Mikes, Mixer, Compressor and Graphic EQ, Reverb and Amp, and Main Speakers

In a medium to large component system, there is normally more than one way to connect some devices. For instance, you can connect the compressor using the main channel's insert jack on your mixer or you can connect it directly in line between the mixer and the power amp. Which is correct? Both! As I pointed out early in this guide, the most important aspect of setting up a P.A. system is understanding the signal flow. With all of the different inserts and outputs on a mixer, it is easy to become confused and interrupt the flow. When this happens, you won't get any sound to your main speakers, so it is important to understand what keeps the signal moving and what can stop it.

In this next configuration, we will connect microphones and instruments to the mixer, add a graphic EQ and compressor to the main mix, make a reverb available to the instruments and mikes, connect the mixer to the amp, and, finally, connect the speakers. The first connection we will make will be to the reverb using the aux send on the mixer. We will assume that the connections to the reverb and delay are unbalanced. Also we will consider that the aux send is monophonic and needs to be connected to a stereo pair of inputs on the reverb unit. In order to make this connection, we will use a tip/sleeve to tip/sleeve 1/4" Y phone cable (See Figure 40: Connecting a Mono Send to Stereo Inputs on the next page). Here we go!

1. Connect the single-sided plug into the mixer's Aux 1 send (this is the mono send) and the other two 1/4" plugs to the stereo input jacks of the reverb. This is diagramed in Figure 40 below.

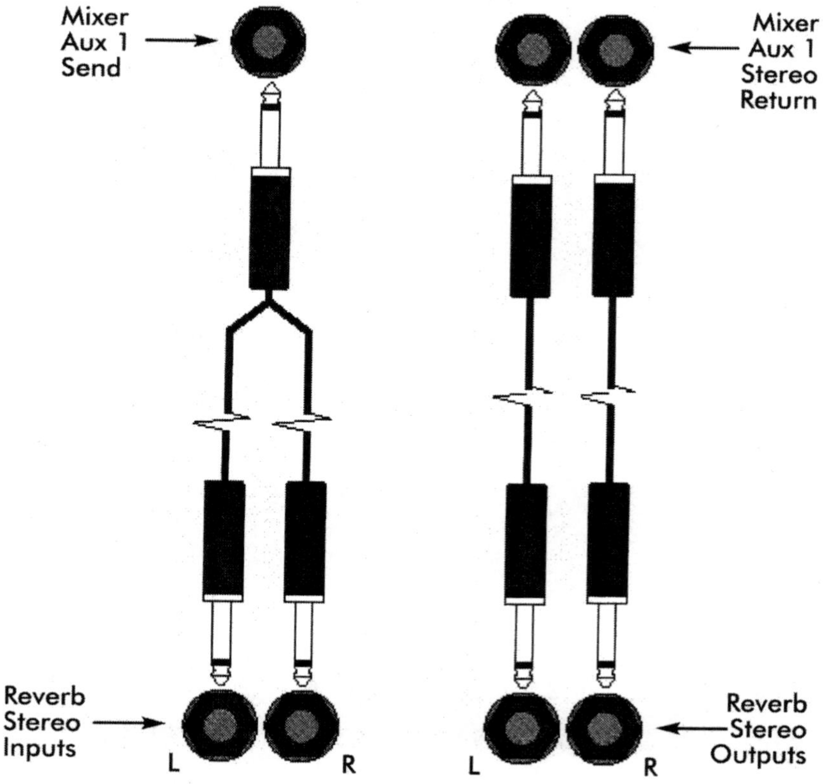

Figure 40: Connecting a Mono Send to Stereo Inputs

2. Connect the stereo output jacks of the reverb unit to the Aux 1 stereo returns on the mixer using two 1/4" tip/sleeve phone cables. In some cases, the reverb unit will have a stereo input but one jack will be marked mono. In this type of set-up, connect a single tip/sleeve 1/4" cable to the Aux 1 send jack and the other 1/4" tip/sleeve plug to the mono input of the reverb.
3. Connecting the graphic EQ and compressor to the main mix outs can be accomplished in either one of two ways: using the main mix inserts (follow Step 3a) or daisy-chaining (follow Step 3b) to the main mix outs. Before we make the connections, however, we need to decide which device will come first, the EQ or compressor. These are the considerations. Remember that the graphic EQ will change the frequency content of the signal, so connecting this first in line will cause the compressor to react to the incoming signal based on the overall level. However, if the compression level is set too high, as the threshold level is crossed and the compressor reduces gain, it may affect how the audience hears certain frequencies. Remember that we don't hear all frequencies equally, so if the EQ is set with a reduction in high-frequency content as the compressor reduces gain, the high frequencies may not be heard since the overall level is being reduced. On the other hand, if low frequencies are boosted, then the compressor may continue to react based on the high energy levels of the low frequencies. If we place the compressor before the EQ, the compressor will reduce gain based on the level coming from the main mix, and then the EQ can be set to balance the overall mix. So in our case, it is best to place the compressor before the graphic EQ.

3a. **Using the main mix inserts** – Using a tip/ring/sleeve (TRS) to (2) tip/sleeve (TS) Y 1/4" phone cable, insert the TRS plug into the mixer's main mix insert jack (we are assuming these are unbalanced connections). Connect the TS send plug into the input of the compressor and the TS return plug into the output of the graphic EQ. Then connect the output of the compressor to the input of the EQ using a tip/sleeve 1/4" phone cable. Repeat this procedure for the main mix insert on the other channel. As you can see, you are sending the mixer's signal to the input of the compressor, and then the compressor's output is sent to the input of the EQ. The EQ's output is then returned to the mixer's insert that will pass the processed signal to the main mix out jacks that will be connected to the amplifier. If you leave out any one of these connections or reverse the send and return plugs, no signal will reach the main mix output jacks. After you have completed these connections, connect the main mix output jacks to the amplifier input jacks with an appropriate cable. In most cases, you will use a 1/4" phone plug cable to make this connection, but XLR cables are also common. If your mixer has 1/4" phone jacks as outputs and your amp has XLR inputs, you will need a special cable to make the proper connection (See Figure 42: 1/4" Tip/Sleeve to XLR Unbalanced Cable). Here I'm going to stress that you get a cable made specifically for this purpose and not use adapter plugs to modify the cable. The reason is that adapters tend to wear with use and the connection may not be solid, which will cause crackling and signal loss in the system. Finally, connect the speaker outputs of the amplifier to the speaker cabinet inputs and you're ready to go. The complete configuration is shown in Figure 42.

Figure 41: 1/4" Tip/Sleeve to XLR Unbalanced Cable

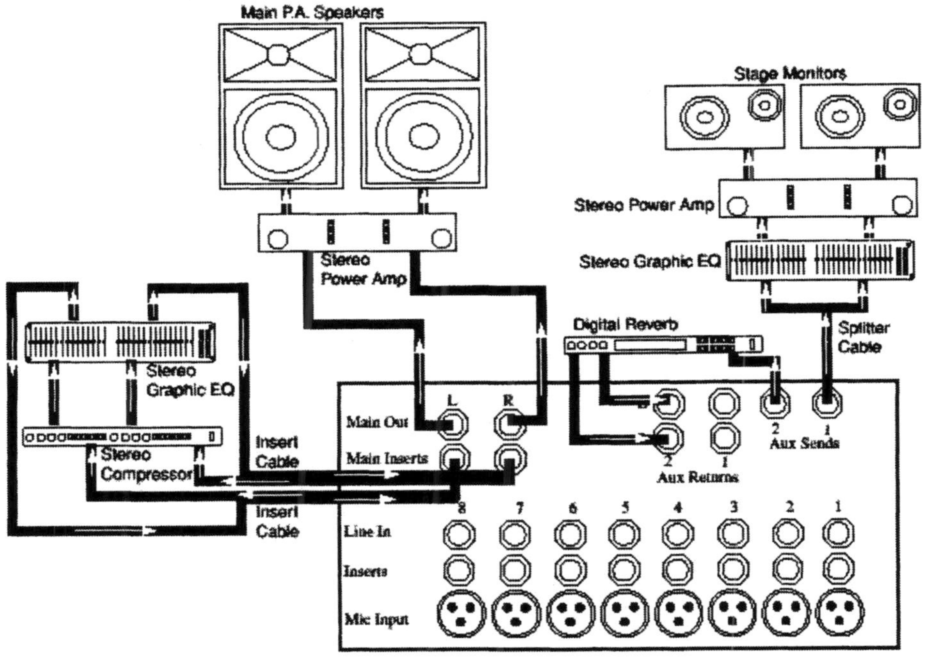

Figure 42: Connecting a Compressor and Graphic EQ With Main Mix Inserts, Digital Reverb to Aux 2, Stage Monitor System to Aux 1, Main Outs to Power Amp and Main Speakers

3b. **Daisy-chaining to the main mix outs** – Another way of connecting the compressor and EQ is by daisy-chaining them to the main mix output jacks. Daisy-chaining is a term used to describe how devices can be connected in a row from output to input. Using an appropriate cable (most likely a 1/4" tip/sleeve), connect the mixer out to the compressor in, the compressor out to graphic EQ in, and then the EQ out to the amplifier in.

Stage Monitor Section: Graphic EQ, Amp, and Stage Monitor Speakers

Connecting a stage monitor system to your mixer is about the same as connecting the main mix outs. The difference is that you use one of the aux sends on the mixer to get the signal to the stage monitor amp and speakers. To make this connection, follow these steps:

1. Use Aux 1 on the mixer as the monitor send. Each channel has an Aux 1 level control that sets the volume of each mike and instrument to be sent to the stage monitor system.
2. Connect the Aux 1 send jack to the input of the graphic EQ.
3. Connect the output of the EQ to the input of the amp. Be sure to use cables that will interface each device properly.
4. Connect the speaker outputs of the amplifier to the stage monitor speaker cabinet inputs. Some stage monitors have an input and output for daisy-chaining multiple stage monitors together from the amplifier. In this type of configuration, you connect the speaker output terminals of the amp to the monitor input of the first stage monitor speaker. Continue to daisy-chain each monitor speaker to the next using a speaker cable. Remember that as you are daisy-chaining the monitor speakers, you are changing the impedance of the system. If the cabinets are wired in parallel, you will reduce the impedance. So be sure not to chain together too many monitor speakers below the rated impedance of the amp. For instance, if the monitor speakers are rated at 16 ohms, daisy-chaining four together will bring the overall impedance down to approximately 4 ohms. Most amps can deliver full power into this load, but check your amp's specification sheet to be absolutely sure.

Powering Up and Shutting Down

This is the part that is usually given the least amount of thought once all the sound system's unit connections are made. In order to avoid damaging your components, especially your speakers, follow this important sequence. The sequence works like this: When any unit is turned on, it will usually emit an audible pop as the electrical circuit is engaged. If the power amp is on at full power and the mixer is then turned on, that pop can cause the power amp to send a powerful transient to the speakers that can damage them. To avoid possible damage, follow these steps in order:

1. Turn on the mixer.
2. Turn on any signal processors connected to the mixer, including reverbs, equalizers, and electronic crossovers.
3. Turn on the power amps.

By turning on the components in this order, no input on any unit will be active and able to receive that nasty pop.

If this makes sense, then you already know you must shut down the system in the reverse order. As each unit is turned off, there may be the same audible pop as the internal components of each unit discharge electricity.

1. Shut down the power amp first to protect the speakers.
2. Then turn off the signal processing.
3. Finally turn off the mixer.

Nice job.

Typical Applications

Speakers With Passive Crossovers

This is a good time to discuss passive crossovers that are built into many speaker systems. The speaker specification sheet will tell you if the speakers you plan to use have passive crossovers built in. A passive crossover is one that is not selectable by the user. These crossovers are built into the speaker enclosure and use frequencies defined by the manufacturer. When a speaker cable is plugged into the input jack of the speaker that has the crossover, it automatically disconnects the different speakers in the enclosure. At this point, each speaker must be powered by a separate amplifier. A common set of inputs on a speaker system would be labeled Normal and Bi-Amp. The normal input is for connecting a single power amp that uses the internal crossover to protect the speakers from damaging frequencies. It also provides the same power to the woofer and the tweeter or horn of the cabinet. When connecting to the bi-amp input, the amp powers only the woofer and a separate power amp is needed to power the high-frequency drivers. In a cabinet that has a 15" full-range woofer and a radial horn, a more powerful amp can be used to drive the low-frequency ranges, and a lesser power amp can be used to power the mid-range horn. Although more expensive in terms of the necessary hardware, this allows the power amp and speaker system to function very efficiently, thus delivering more usable power to the speakers and sound to the audience.

Bi- or Tri-Amping

These are expensive propositions because they require more than one power amp. The output of the mixer is connected to the input of an electronic crossover. The crossover allows for the selection of specific frequency ranges that will be connected to amps and then ultimately the speaker system. A common bi-amp speaker system will consist of a low-frequency driver, usually a 15" or 18" speaker and a mid-range/high-frequency cabinet. The crossover is set so that only the frequencies below 100 Hz are sent to the amp powering the low-frequency cabinets. The second output of the crossover sends all frequencies above 100 Hz to the mid-range/high-frequency speaker amp. Tri-amping uses the same principle but divides the range into lows, mids, and highs. Here three power amps will be needed to power the three different speaker cabinets. See Figure 43 for a diagram of this configuration. The actual settings on the crossover will be based on the frequency response ratings on the speakers. Don't try to compensate for a lack of bass by boosting the low EQ 12 dB at 60 Hz if the speaker can only respond to 100 Hz. This will cause the power amp to work harder, and no significant bass will be realized unless the speaker system is capable of reproducing those frequencies. The result could be damaged speakers, so make sure you have the right tools for the job.

One bright side to the additional expense is that you won't need amps of equal power in this situation, so some money can be saved. The rule to follow is that the low frequencies will need the most power, then the mids and highs. How much power you need is based on the size of the rooms you play or if you play outdoors.

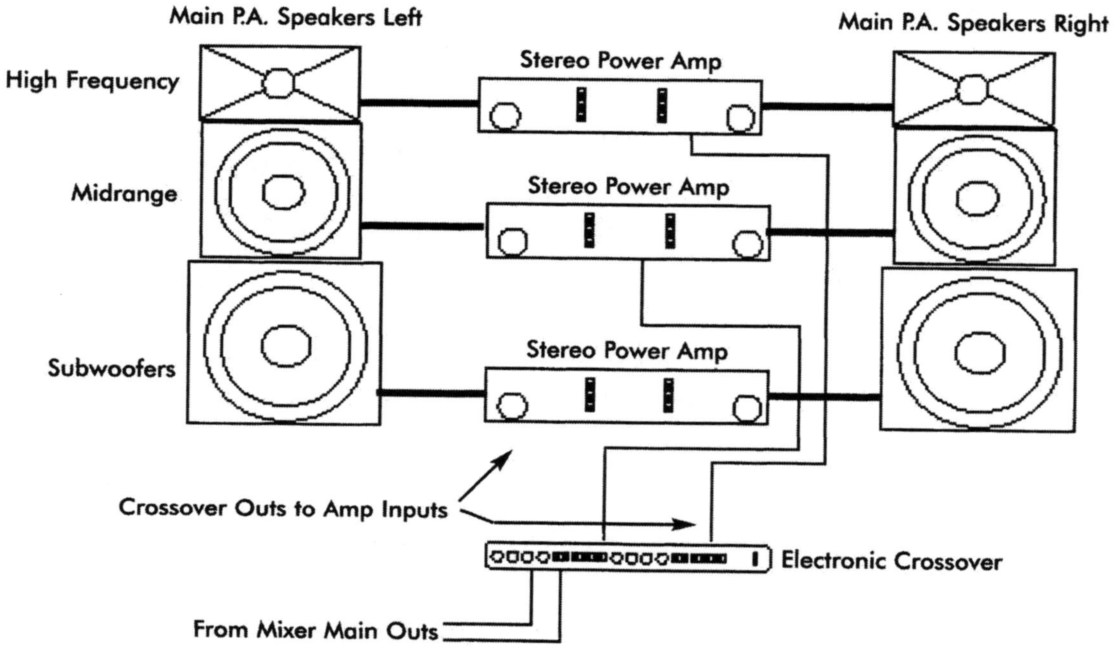

Figure 43: Tri-Amp Configuration With Electronic Crossover

Dealing With Different Room Sizes and Acoustic Characteristics

One thing you can count on is that no two playing environments will be exactly the same. You will probably play outside, in small clubs, and in large function rooms. Each one of these situations will call for some creativity on your part to get the best sound possible. Outside is probably the most difficult because there is no natural reverb and the sound is not contained as it is in a closed room. Sound emanating from a sound system outside just keeps traveling with no reflections off nearby walls. The sound can be dry and the bass may sound thin. In this type of performance area, you will need speakers capable of reproducing very low frequencies and will also need some kind of signal processing to provide reverb and warmth. On a windy day, microphones will howl if you don't use a wind screen. Stage monitors will also sound different since there will not be a nearby wall or ceiling to reflect the sound back into the performance area. Feedback can be a real problem here since volume levels normally need to be higher outside. In almost all cases, your most important signal processor will become your graphic equalizer because it will allow you to contour the sound to simulate a closed space.

Small rooms and clubs have a different set of problems; the hardest one to overcome is equalization. Nine times out of ten, you will set up the P.A. with no people present. The problem here is that people are just as much a part of the acoustical environment as are chairs, carpeting, and acoustic ceiling tiles. They absorb certain frequencies and block others from passing through to the back of the room. This is most noticeable with the upper mid and high frequencies. The best solution for this is to get your speakers up high, around or above the audience's ear level. If you are setting up on a stage that is three feet high, this will help in getting the speakers up to their proper height. If there is no stage, then stacking speakers on tables or putting the smaller speakers on stands will help get them high enough so the crowd will have a minimum effect on the sound quality. Stages themselves will present a problem with the microphones. Since most stages are hollow below, they act like large drums when you walk on them. What happens is that the stage vibrates when you walk on it; that vibration can be passed up into the mike through the microphone stand. One part of solving this problem is to use the mike stand that has the least contact with the stage. This can be done by using a stand with a tripod base instead of a large, flat iron one. This isolates the total area in contact with the floor, thus reducing the transmission of the vibration to the mike. Another way to reduce this effect is with a shock mount mike holder. This mounts the mike on the stand by suspending it rather than screwing it directly to the stand post. Using a small piece of carpet can also help reduce the vibration passing from the floor to the mike.

One thing is sure: You will encounter all types of acoustical problems as you move to different performing venues. As you encounter problems, try to identify why the sound is less than ideal, and then go about finding the solution to fix it. For instance, another way to get rid of some of the low-frequency stage problems discussed earlier is to use a low-frequency cut filter (sometimes included as a button on some mixers) that will roll off frequencies below 75 Hz at 18 dB per octave. Since vocals are not in that range, this will have minimal effect on the vocal quality while getting rid of the rumble from the stage. Remember to use your ears—listen, listen, listen—before you start twirling knobs or moving things around the room.

Standing Waves

What is a standing wave? It is a low-frequency content sound that will start at one end of a square or rectangular room, hit the opposite wall, and reflect back to the sound source. As additional sound waves are generated, this back-and-forth reflection tends to reinforce certain low frequencies and also tends to create a booming bass sound in certain spots in the room. The most obvious place this occurs is in a room like a high school gym. The walls are concrete, the floor is wood, and the room is rectangular. I think there are bass notes still going in my old high school gym from 30 years ago!

For the most part, standing waves in a room like this will exist no matter what you do. But you can help reduce the effect by changing the placement of the main speaker system. By turning the speakers at an angle to the back wall, the initial sound waves will hit the side walls first and reflect on an angle to the opposite side of the room. If you play pool (or billiards), you can see this effect by the way a cue ball bounces from one rail to the next. If you stand at the long end of the table and hit the cue ball to the far rail, it will continue to bounce back and forth in a straight line. This is what the standing wave will do if the speakers are facing directly at the back wall. Now if you strike the cue ball to hit one of the side rails, the ball will bounce off of a number of rails before it returns to the end of the table from where you first hit it. By facing your speakers slightly towards a side wall, the sound is diffused by creating more reflections and the standing wave is reduced. The key word here is "reduced," not "eliminated." There are a number of complicated acoustical interactions going on among the sound, walls, floor, and ceiling that cause a room to sound a certain way. That's why it costs more money to design a concert hall than a high school gym!

Dealing With Mike Feedback and Other Unwanted Noises

The main reason a P.A. system will produce feedback is due to main speaker or stage monitor placement. Any time sound from the system is permitted to re-enter a microphone, a feedback loop will inevitably start. Using a directional microphone will help reduce the possibility of feedback but will not be able to eliminate it altogether if the speaker placement is poor. As discussed in the Microphone Polar Pattern section, directional microphones have areas off axis that offer greater frequency rejection than others. When placing stage monitors, this "dead" spot on the mike should be the area where the monitor is pointing. This won't completely defeat feedback if the monitor level is too high. The high level sound coming from the monitor will simply wrap around the mike capsule and start feeding back.

Another reason for feedback is too much high-frequency EQ added to the monitor system. Although this tends to make the monitors sound crisp, it will, in most cases, cause feedback when the gain is increased. Stage monitors are there to keep the band together, and there will be some compromises with the sound quality. If the vocalist likes to hear a crisp, bright sound in the monitors, the level will usually have to be lower than if some of the high end is rolled off. If, on the other hand, the monitors have to be loud, then some of the high end will have to be rolled off to prevent the feedback. This is where the saying, "You can't please all of the people all of the time," really hits home.

Chapter Eight

Troubleshooting

What do you do when you've finished setting up the system and things don't work or distortion comes from the system? Tear it all down and start all over? Hardly. What you need to do is figure out what is causing the problem. For instance, if there is no sound coming from the system at all, first check to see if the mixer, signal processors, crossovers, and power amps are on. All of these units have pilot lights (usually LEDs) that show they are on. Next, make sure the volume controls are turned up in the normal operating range. If this checks out, shut down all of these units in the proper order and check all of the speaker cables to make sure they are fully seated and connected. If this, too, proves not to be the problem, check to see if the cables coming from the mixer are connected properly to signal processors that are connected to the inserts or main mix outputs.

Another problem may be speaker distortion on one side of the system. To check the speakers, simply swap the sides of the power amp. If the distortion stays on the same side, it is safe to say you have bad speakers. If it switches to the other side, you probably have a problem with the power amp or one of the other components. It could be that one side is being overdriven or a cable, signal processor, or mixer may be defective.

It takes only a little bit of logical thinking to troubleshoot most sound systems. If you understand the signal flow (remember that from the start of this guide?), you can diagnose, trace, and fix most of the problems.

Conclusion

Well, that about does it. This book has given you a good foundation in live sound reinforcement, but the only way now to become truly proficient at using the equipment is to get out there and play in front of people, much the same way you practice and play an instrument. When you practice, you have time to go back over your mistakes, play at different tempos, and work out fingerings. But once you're on stage, you perform, you get excited, and if you make a mistake, you just keep on going. The same thing holds true for using your P.A. It is the system that helps deliver the energy and sound of your band to the audience. Prepare well in advance and you'll deliver the very best sound possible at the gig. Preparation before the performance will save you time in set-up and give you confidence in your system. Use a cable tester to check all of your connecting cables regularly so you won't have to track down a bad one when you're on the job. Make sure that if your equipment uses fuses, you carry a supply of the proper ratings with you at all times. Never use a fuse of a higher rating than specified by the equipment. You could severely damage the gear and could cause a fire! Have confidence, use your ears, and, most of all, make music! Remember that the equipment is here to serve music-making, not the other way around.

Manufacturer Web Sites of Interest

The following is a useful list of manufacturer Web sites. These sites are updated regularly, and the addresses sometimes change if sites undergo major overhauls. Don't worry though; if this happens, the sites will usually give you the new addresses. I use the Web quite a bit to compare specs among products and companies. In some cases, you can find out suggested retail prices to give you an idea of what a piece of gear costs.

DBX Professional Products
www.dbxpro.com

JBL Professional Products
www.jblpro.com

DOD
www.dod.com

Shure
www.shure.com

Electrovoice
www.electrovoice.com

Fender
www.fender.com

Peavey
www.peavey.com

AKG acoustics
www.akg-acoustics.com

Lexicon
www.lexicon.com

Alesis
www.alesis.com

SoundCraft
www.soundcraft.com

Mackie
www.mackie.com